MW00436319

SIMON PETER:
his life and works

By Dr. Jerry Haughton

Jesus replied, "Blessed are you, Simon son of Jonah, for this was not revealed to you by man, but my Father in heaven. And I tell you that you are Peter, and on this rock I will build my church, and the gates of Hades will not overcome it."

Matthew 16:17,18

Amazon Books

Table of Contents

INTRODUCTION

Simon Peter was a follower of Jesus Christ that tried to be obedient, but often blundered. He was a sincere but impulsive person who often caused problems. Many believers identify with his faith and hopes, as well as his doubts and confusion. For this reason, his life and writings are a good source of study for all who follow Christ. These thirty studies are not academic; but they are *biblical* and *practical* and can serve as daily devotions for a month or a series of sermons for seven months. Each takes about 30 minutes to read.

Hermeneutics is the science of interpreting Scripture. One rule is: "There is only *one correct interpretation* of a Scripture, but *many applications.*" This concept is followed throughout the study. I draw from the experiences of Simon Peter to find truths that are applicable to every Christian's life.

Several Church Fathers: Papias, c.120; Irenaeus, c.180; Clement of Rome, c.195, claim that the apostle Peter *dictated* his gospel account to Mark, so I will use it as the primary source. Matthew, Luke and John will be consulted only where Mark does not record his words or deeds. The Book of Acts recounts Peter's exploits from Pentecost to the Apostolic Council in Jerusalem, 49 A.D. The Church Fathers tell us of his death at Rome c. 66 A.D.

You should read the passage of Scripture in several translations and then the **narrative**. Reflect on the **applications** drawn from the passage and then apply the truths to your own life.

1 PETER'S BACKGROUND
Read: John 1:35-44

Jesus' public ministry began with his baptism by John the Baptizer in 27 or 28 A.D. The next day Andrew introduced Simon Peter to Jesus. Andrew had been a disciple of the Baptizer and was expecting the Jewish Messiah, so he *immediately* recognized Jesus as that person. It would take Simon Peter about another year before he reached the same conclusion.

Narrative

We do not have much biographical data on Simon, but we can deduce enough to have a general description.

* He was probably near the same age as Jesus, early or mid-thirties at the time of his call. His complexion was dark from working outside and he was strong because of pulling the fishnets.

* We know he had a wife, but there is no mention of his parents, children, aunts/uncles, cousins. (Since it was unusual for a Jewish man to be unmarried, we must assume that all the disciples had wives, and possibly children; however, we do not know the names of their family members.) Peter probably had an extended family of 50 to 100 persons. How did they react to his commitment to Jesus as the Messiah?

* Simon and Andrew grew up in Bethsaida. It was at the north end of the Sea of Galilee and on the major trade route from Egypt to Damascus and beyond. Greek and Roman cultures were dominant due to a large Gentile population.

* Simon most likely had a synagogue education. He learned the OT stories as well as to read, write and do some math. He knew some conversational Greek, but Aramaic was his native language.

* He was a fisherman by trade. Andrew, James and John were his business partners. They made an

adequate living by selling the catch every morning in the marketplace of Capernaum, a small Jewish community on the west-central part of Galilee.

Jesus immediately read the personality of Simon, so he gave him a new name: Peter, which means "rock." It was common for rabbis to give characterizing names to their disciples. The Jewish people accepted this practice due to the prophetic nature of the teacher.

Application

* Andrew's *method of witnessing* of Christ was natural. It is known as life-style evangelism. Any other approach is open to manipulation. Andrew did not need to learn steps to lead others to Christ, he just spoke of what he believed to his brother. Family members are probably the most difficult to reach because they know all our weaknesses. Nevertheless, Andrew opened the door for his brother Simon, even though the latter did not step through it at this time. It is enough to present the Gospel and allow time for the Holy Spirit to bring it to completion (I Cor.3:5,6). If a person shows no interest in spiritual matters in the years to come it means that the Spirit did not do a work of conviction of sin to produce repentance. Why the Spirit regenerates some and not others is a *mystery*. Jesus said, "The Spirit is like the wind, it blows where it wills" Jn3:8. We see this among family and friends. Some are saved and others are lost even though they have the same physical opportunities.

* The Lord *knows* each one of his followers to the center of their being. He calls us by our spiritual name and we follow him (Jn.10:3b). Our parents gave us a name they hoped would reflect our character, but the Lord gives us a new name when we are born into his family to show the true nature of our character (Rev.2:17).

* The fact that the Lord took a man like Peter, who had no standing in the world, indicates that he *can use anyone* who *commits* to him. No one, regardless of their

common status, should claim that s/he is unable to serve the Lord. In fact, the Lord works by paradox; he most often uses people who are not recognized by the world as great in any way (I Cor.1:26--29).

2   PETER'S FIRST STEP OF FAITH
Read: Luke 5:1-11

Narrative
About eight months after Peter was introduced to Jesus, they had another encounter with him. By this time Jesus had cleared the Temple (Jn.2:12-22) and had been rejected at the synagogue of Nazareth, causing him to move to Capernaum, where Simon Peter lived. Jesus had preached the Sermon on the Mount on one of the local hillsides and Peter probably heard it or heard others talk about it.

Jesus' popularity (or notoriety) had spread so that thousands wanted to hear him. On one occasion He asked to use Peter's boat so that he could push off shore from the crowd to teach them. Peter navigated the boat and had to hear the sermon. When Jesus finished he told Peter where to cast his nets so that he could make a catch. (This was the rent Jesus paid for the boat use.)

Peter protested that they had fished all night and caught nothing, but he did so anyway and the nets were so filled that he could not pull in the catch. This event spoke to Peter more than the sermon, for he realized that Jesus knew all things, even his heart. So Peter confessed that he was a sinful man and made a commitment to follow Christ.

Application
  *   Simon *confessed* that he was a sinner. No one

acknowledges Christ as Savior until s/he realizes that they have violated God's holy nature. The Ten Commandments are the expression of God's moral standard. Sinners usually live in denial and can only be brought to know that they have offended God by the work of the Holy Spirit. Otherwise they continue to make excuses for their sinful behavior. Jesus said, "Light has come into the world, but men loved darkness instead of light because their deeds were evil" Jn.3:19. Sinners' love their sins and will not leave them of their own will.

    *   Not all persons who follow Jesus Christ are required to leave their source of livelihood. Later, Peter reminded Jesus that they had left a lucrative business to be his disciples (Mk.10:28-31). Notice, Jesus did not promise to make them wealthy because of their commitment, rather he promised *spiritual blessings* that far exceed the material things they left behind. Every believer has been "blessed with every spiritual blessing" Eph.1:3. This means that none of us are lacking in a spiritual gift(s). Paul confessed that his spiritual blessings far exceeded his material belongings (Phil.3:7-9). If a person does continue in the same business after conversion, the biblical principle of honesty should change his business practices. Holiness is not becoming more religious, it is letting truth and honesty control every facet of our daily life (Ex.19).

3 AN EYEWITNESS OF MIRACLES
Read: Mark 1:21-34

Narrative

How *blessed* to have lived in the Jewish nation at the time of Christ, or to have been at the Sea of Galilee, or to have lived in Capernaum, but especially to have Jesus come to your home for dinner after worship in the synagogue. All this happened to Simon Peter.

Jesus preached his first sermon in the synagogue at Nazareth. When he read Isaiah 61:1-2a and claimed its fulfillment, they tried to throw him off a cliff because they knew he was declaring himself to be the Messiah. He escaped somehow and moved to Capernaum and began teaching in the synagogue there.

The synagogue at Gamla, just 6 miles from Capernaum has been excavated. It was 84 by 56 feet. People were seated around three sides on five stair-steps. As many as 430 could attend a service. The floor was dirt with four tiles in the center where the reader of Scripture stood. Jesus probably taught here.

What a privilege to have heard Jesus preach and teach. He was unlike all the other rabbis, in that, it was *new*. Every Sabbath the rabbis taught in the local synagogue. These men had been to rabbinic school (seminary) and learned how to interpret Scripture. They often quoted from commentaries of other famous rabbis to reinforce their interpretation, however, their messages were only informed *opinions* of what any passage meant.

When Jesus preached there was a difference; he did not quote from any rabbis. He spoke as one having *authority*, that is, he knew absolutely the true meaning of every passage of Scripture. This is evident in the Sermon on the Mount: "You have heard that it was said...but I tell you." In brief, he was refuting all the interpretations of other rabbis before him and giving the correct interpretation.

Peter, along with the other disciples, had the privilege of hearing these unique insights into Scripture and often asked questions. Jesus told them that they had been given special privileges and that they were hearing truths that OT prophets longed to know (Mt.13:10-12, 16,17). And because they were so special they had a greater responsibility to teach these new truths to others (Mt.13:51,52).

Peter was also an eyewitness to the miracles Jesus' performed. A miracle is an exception to natural law. When Jesus exercised *authority over nature* the results were instantaneous and successful. No incantations or lapse of time was needed. Those who stood near saw the change of condition of those Jesus healed. In the synagogue at Capernaum a demon was driven from a man (who was probably disturbing the service) by Jesus' orders. Wow! After the service Jesus went home with Peter and healed his mother-in-law of a fever. Wow! Later, Peter witnessed the healing of the woman bleeding to death and a dead girl being raised to life (Mk.5:30-34;37-43). Wow! He was also in the boat with the disciples when a severe storm threatened and Jesus spoke to the wind and waves and all was immediately calm (Mk.4:35-41). Wow!

These miracles *authenticated* the claim of Jesus to be God in flesh. Peter saw these miracles (2 Pet.1:16) and later made the confession that Jesus was the Messiah. The *cumulative effect* of Jesus' teachings and miracles *convinced* Peter that Jesus was God.

Application

* Which preacher is right? Over a lifetime a church member hears many pastors. They all have a different style and emphasis. It can be confusing for members when they detect contradictions between pastors. So-and-so said this, but you do not have the same view. Why? The simple answer is: one of them knows more than the other one (the same reason some doctors are better than others or some lawyers are better than others). The pastor who has a better understanding of Scripture is the one the church member should believe. If members listen carefully, over a period of years they ought to be able to discern which preaching is more faithful to the whole message of the Bible.   On a spiritual level, some pastors are more spiritually attuned than others. They usually pray and study more over a passage than the other pastors.

When Christians hear the deeper truths of the Faith they often ask, "Why didn't our previous pastors tell us these things?" The answer is: Either they did not know them or did not believe them, or they were cautious lest church members take offense to the new teaching and be upset.

* Church members of this day have been infected with the spirit of the age, which is: all truth claims are *equal*. People are created equal because they are in the image of God (Acts 17:26, 29a), but all beliefs are not equal. Some are better than others because they agree with reality. There is a desperate need for *spiritual discernment* among Christians. A naïve pluralism pervades our society; therefore, people resist any message that distinguishes truth from error, which is *basic* to biblical preaching. If a pastor sounds authoritative it might be because he knows the truth. Those who do not like the message will attack the messenger. If it is not a direct criticism of the pastor himself, it can be of his family. Those who were offended by Jesus often attacked his lifestyle (e.g. he eats and drinks with sinners, or he plucks grain on the Sabbath and eats it, and so forth).

I have preached with authority from the beginning; and have become more authoritative as the years passed because I know who I am and what I believe. Criticism from others only reveals to me where they are spiritually and does not affect my views or style. One of the greatest compliments was paid to me at a church dinner when one member commented how much she liked the sermon, then immediately across the table a woman said, "And he means it too." Thank God my people sense that I am speaking the word of God and not just my opinion. Some members have left who did not like my authoritative preaching, but others have been drawn to it.

* What convinced the reader to believe that Jesus is God and trust him as Savior? You did not hear Jesus teach or see him heal. In fact, miracles no longer take place on the same order of those performed by Jesus. Rather, a person now believes because someone was faithful in telling the Gospel story (Jn.20:28-31) and the Holy Spirit regenerated you. Jesus said, "Blessed are those who have not seen and yet have come to believe" Jn.20:29.

4 CHOSEN AND SENT
Read: Mark 3:7,13-19

Narrative

By this time in Jesus' ministry large crowds (thousands) were following him, mostly for his miracles. On this occasion he called out from the crowd twelve men to be his disciples. This meant that they were to live and travel with him, and be prepared to go out preaching his message with his authority.

He chose twelve because they, like the twelve sons of Jacob that constituted Israel, would constitute the new Israel, the Church. The twenty-four elders in the book of Revelation represent OT and NT believers in Heaven (Rev.4:9,10).

Jesus chose these twelve men in particular from the crowd of several thousand, not because they had theological training or were more intelligent or had better morals than others. Just as God chose Israel because of his love for them above other nations (Deut.7:7,8), Jesus chose these twelve because he loved them in a way that he did not love the rest. It might have been awkward for Jesus to call out the names from the crowd, but these twelve responded to his call because they sensed on a deeper level that he was the Messiah. They proved to be teachable and willing to obey. Others applied for the position of disciple but were not willing to leave all to join his ministry (Mt.8:18-22). A scribe said he would follow Jesus everywhere, but as often is the case with Jesus, but he did not address the statement of the person, rather he looked deep into his heart and said "no". He knew this man would not leave his comfortable life. The next man claimed that he would follow after he buried his father. Jesus again went to the heart of the matter and said, "no." This would-be disciple must put spiritual matters before earthly responsibilities.

Even though Jesus did not call any women as disciples, some of them chose to follow him for the next two years of his ministry (Lk.8:1-3). They traveled separately from the twelve men in order to avoid every appearance of evil. For the past two thousand years women have *not* served in the leadership of churches, but recently women have been accepted as pastors in churches that ignore Scripture. Women have usually have been faithful in support ministries.

After several months of learning from Jesus and seeing how he lived, the disciples were ready to be sent on a short term mission (Mk.6:6b-13). He gave them the following instructions:

* Go out with a companion for encouragement and to confirm the witness. Peter and John ministered together after the Jesus' resurrection.

* They took no provisions to show their dependence on the Lord.

* Those who benefited by their ministry were to support the disciples.

* They were not to settle in one place for very long.

* If their ministry was rejected by a town, they were to shake the dust off their clothes as a sign of God's judgment on the people there. (In the parallel reading in Matthew 10:11-13, the disciples were to find a *person of peace* in the village that the Lord had already prepared to receive their message and stay in that home. This principle is still used today.)

* They were to anoint the sick with oil, which symbolized the Holy Spirit, as a means of healing.

Their impact was so great that King Herod in Jerusalem heard and became concerned. When the disciples returned they reported to Jesus the success they had on mission, and he led them to a quiet place of retreat (vss.30,31).

Application

* Everyone who confesses Jesus as Savior is to become a disciple (learner). We were chosen in the same sense as the original disciples: he loved us (Eph.1:4). None of us were qualified. We are to spend time with Jesus by being in the word and at prayer so that we are prepared to give a good witness to those around us. We have a problem, however, that the first disciples did not have: How do you witness to people who have already heard some version of the gospel and rejected it? Most people in Western societies have turned away from the Gospel and are secularists or atheists. The only place the Church is growing is in countries where the Gospel has never been preached.

* The guidelines Jesus laid down for these first disciples did *not* apply to missionaries thereafter. Paul did not follow them when he went on his mission travels, except finding the person of peace to stay with. Missionaries who are sent out by a denominational board of missions have their needs well provided for. On the other hand, faith missionaries have to raise their own support and often struggle to meet basic needs. If we do not go on mission we are responsible for searching out missionaries that we can personally

support. This part of what it means to lay up treasures in heaven. My wife and I have given financial support to faith missionaries over the years and have been greatly blessed by hearing their stories of how the Lord used them.

* We should *multiply* our spiritual life by *mentoring* believers who want to learn biblical truths in order to teach others. Paul told Timothy, "And the things you have heard from me say in the presence of many witnesses entrust to reliable men who will also be qualified to teach others" 2 Tim.2:2. I was privileged to teach in a Christian college for fifteen years and had young men and women develop an affinity for my teachings and me. They came to the church I pastored, as well as to my home for personal interaction. Some defected along the way like Judas did with Jesus and Demas did with Paul, but most have been faithful to what I taught. I rejoice when I hear of their ministries.

5 PERSONALITY: TYPE A
Read: Mt.14:22-33

Narrative
For Jesus to walk on water is believable because he is God, but for Peter to think that he could do the same is incredible. This event shows that Peter was a daring person. None of the other disciples thought about getting out of the boat and trying it. Four of these men were fishermen and knew the dangers of the sea during a storm. Seeing Jesus walking on the water caused Peter to disregard common sense. He actually got out of the boat and his feet met liquid that supported his body and he walked toward Jesus. When he came to his

senses and realized what he was doing, he sank and Jesus had to lift him up and place him in the boat. No man had walked on water before, and no man since.

What kind of personality does a man have in order to do something like this? People have different personalities, even in the same family. Parents who have more than one child are amazed at how opposite their children are. Peter was unusual, maybe unstable in our estimation. His brother Andrew was probably the opposite.

Temperament is the raw material out of which personality is formed. It is the mental and emotional nature that is passed genetically from our parents. From this clay the vessel is shaped by interaction with family, friends, environment, authority figures during a child's formative years. The writer of Proverbs alludes to this when he said, "Train up a child according to his way (i.e. temperament) and when he is mature he will not depart from it" (paraphrase of 22:6). Good parents take into account the temperament in each child and adapt their training to shape the child's personality. A proverb: "As the twig is bent the tree will grow."

A *pattern emerges* throughout the Gospels that reveal the personality of Peter. We do not have any information about his rearing, but we learn from his interactions with Jesus and the other disciples what his personality was like. Here are a few situations:

He chided Jesus, "Everyone is searching for you [Jesus]." Mk.1:37

* was abrupt, "Go away from me Lord, for I am a sinful man." Lk.5:8

* was absurd, "Lord, if it is you, command me to come to you on the water." Mk.8:29

* was spiritually sensitive, "You are the Christ." Mk.8:29

* was effusive, "Never Lord. This shall never happen to you!" Mt. 16:22.

* was brazen, "Rabbi, it is good for us to be here, let us make three dwellings." Mk.9:5

* complained, "Look, we have left everything and followed you." Mk.10:28

* was curious, "Rabbi, look! The fig tree you cursed has withered." Mk.11;21

* over reacted, "You will never wash my feet...Lord, not my feet only but also my hands and my head" Jn.13:8,9

* boasted, "Even though all become deserters, I will not." Mk.14:29

* was inquisitive, "Who is the betrayer?" Jn.13:24

* was rash: Simon Peter drew the sword and "cut off the right ear of the high priest's servant," Jn.18:10

* was bold: "Then Simon Peter came and went into the tomb..." Jn.20:6a.

What sense does the reader get from these statements of Peter? He was certainly the most outspoken of the disciples. Blurting out whatever came to mind without thinking was a habit. He also rushed into situations without caution. Sometimes a good observer, but at other times he made stupid comments. His attitude and disposition was rude and domineering. I am amazed that none of the other disciples challenged him in a physical altercation like men do when boundaries are crossed. His brother Andrew seems completely passive, in that, he did not say anything worth recording in the Gospels.

Character is the mental and moral qualities that distinguish one person from another. We say that a person has good character qualities or bad character qualities, thus evaluating them. Most people have a mixture. Peter was such a person. He definitely became the leader of the band of disciples because he was a take control type of person. His actions might be wrong, but he was never in doubt about what he did.

Jesus knew Simon Peter's personality when he chose him to be a disciple (Jn.2:25). He also knew that the personality of Peter would be *transformed* by the teaching and time he spent with him. After Pentecost, when Peter was filled with the Holy Spirit, his aggressive personality was turned into a boldness for the Lord that defied governing authorities, the same ones who had put Jesus to death only six weeks earlier (Acts 4:8-13,19,29; 5:33).

Application

    * This story has often been used as an *analogy* of the Christian life. The storm represents the problems we face, but if we look to Jesus we should rise above them, however, if we take our eyes off Jesus, we too will sink beneath the adversities of life. Even then, if we call on him, he will take us to the safety of the ship. In actuality it is a true story that recounts why the apostles came to believe that Jesus was the Son of God. To use it as an analogy of the Christian life is to teach something that is not true. When Jesus does not magically rescue us from our problems we are prone to think that Christianity doesn't work. The truth is: Jesus is with us *through* life's problems, but he does not rescue us from them. He goes through them with us.

    * Psychology 101 teaches that one's personality changes very little, if at all. But this does not take into account the power of the Holy Spirit working in a person.

    David stated that the Lord knew him from the time of his conception and shaped his temperament (Ps.139:13-16). The *genetic* makeup of parents has more impact on children than the environment in which they are reared. The Lord also told Jeremiah, "Before I formed you in the womb I knew you, before you were born I set you apart; I appointed you as a prophet to the nations" 1;4,5.

    This is true of each believer, in that, the Lord knew us before we were born. He knows our weaknesses and fears right now that are holding us back from doing his work. Regardless of our temperament and how our personality was shaped, he can *transform* its negative qualities into positive ones that he can use in the kingdom. The reader might think that his peculiar personality is a hindrance to the Lord doing a work through him, but not so. We need to experience the freedom of the Spirit. When any personality is filled with the Holy Spirit, it can meet a need for a certain time and place that only the Lord knows.

I know a man who was told repeatedly by his father that he was "hard headed." There was a stubborn streak in his personality. When he became a man he entered the ministry. The Lord used this negative trait to cause him to resist compromise of the Word as well as to disregard the criticisms of others. (All pastors have feet of clay.) A strong personality is needed to pastor churches filled with immature Christians. As a result of the Spirit filling his life he can stand strong for Truth, but if he quenches the Spirit he is a difficult person to be around. And yet, the Lord still loves him when he fails and renews him. We often tell the Lord how much we love him, but we need to hear the Lord telling us how much he loves us regardless of our personality quirks (more about this later).

6 A GREAT CONFESSION
Read: Mark 8:27-33

Narrative
This retreat of Jesus and the disciples to the hillside of Mt. Hermon marks a turning point in Jesus' ministry. He had been rejected in Jerusalem and Galilee. The expectation of the masses that he would be the King and provide for their physical needs had diminished. Most were not interested in his spiritual truths. So, he intentionally took his disciples to a Gentile region to learn if they understood who he is.

The masses regarded him only as another

prophet. This is where Jesus began his questioning. He asked: "Who do people say I am?" They replied, "Some say John the Baptist, others say Elijah; and still others, one of the prophets (e.g. Jeremiah)."

"But what about you?" he asked, "Who do you say I am?" The "you" is emphatic by its place in the question, and it is second person plural, meaning it was directed at *all* the disciples. Was there a pause with the disciples looking at one another to see who would answer first? Or, did Peter, in his characteristic way, answer impulsively? I think the answer exploded out of his mouth: "You are the Messiah."

To confess Jesus as the Christ meant to own and acknowledge that he is God in flesh. This was a radical statement then, as it is now. The disciples had spent a year and a half hearing the teachings of Jesus and seeing the miracles he performed. By degrees they were realizing that he was the Messiah, but it was hard because of their preconceived notions that he was to be a conquering king like David who would drive out the Romans.

We turn now to Matthew 16:17-20 to see the rest of the story.

Jesus received the confession as truth, then replied, "Blessed are you Simon, son of Jonah, for this was not revealed to you by man, but by my Father in heaven." His confession was not based on human reason, it was a *revelation* from God.

Now Jesus has the *foundation* of his ministry. Peter's confession is the *basis* for the Church. Up to this point Jesus had spoken about the Kingdom of God, but now he speaks of the Church. The Kingdom is spiritual, but the Church is a physical reality. Jesus taught that the Kingdom (rule of God) is in the human heart. The Church, however, is believers who gather regularly for worship at a local place. They are the "called out ones" from the larger community.

Jesus then gave the keys of the kingdom to Peter. Nothing is said here about Peter being a Pope, nor is

there a distinction between *petros* and *petra,* as
Protestants teach, because Jesus spoke Aramaic and
used *kepha* in both references. Peter was given the
authority to preach and he *exercised* it at Pentecost. The
head steward of a household carried the keys on his
shoulders as a sign of authority (Isa.22:22). The first
member of the Church is to be *first among equals* (I
Pet.5:1). There is nothing here declaring that Peter is a
priest. In fact, the apostles were not priests. The word
priest is never used in the NT regarding a minister.
Peter is the apostle that emphasized: "every believer is
a priest that offers sacrifices to God." The "whole
church is a priesthood, a holy nation" I Pet. 2:5,9. Only
in the book of Hebrews is the word priest used, and that
is speaking of Jesus as our High Priest. The priestly
system of the RC, the EO, and the Anglican/Episcopal
denominations is based on a *false* premise---belief that a
select group had the power to consecrate the elements
of Communion and to forgive sins. Jesus would have
none of it if he were walking the earth today, in fact, he
would clear out the Vatican as he did the Jewish Temple.
(Read Gary Wills' book: WHY PRIESTS? A Failing
Tradition.) The priestly rituals are a twisted portrayal of
Christianity. The three great truths recovered by the
Reformation were: Justification by faith apart from good
works; the sufficiency of Scripture alone apart from
tradition; and the priesthood of all believers without a
church priesthood. This latter one is often forgotten,
but is probably the most important in refuting the RC,
EO and Anglican systems of religion.

   Peter's confession: "You are the Christ, the Son of
the living God," is repeated by everyone who enters the
Church. The keys are the declaration of the gospel
message that opens the door of salvation for sinners to
repent. Although the Church was established at this
time it must remain in obscurity until the Spirit comes
at Pentecost.

Application

   *   World religions often regard Jesus as a prophet (e.g. Islam, Buddhism). If this is true, it means that his death was only a martyrdom and not an atonement for sin. But worst, it denies who he claimed to be--God in human flesh. Muslims regard Jesus as a great prophet, but cannot accept him as God's son. They cannot grasp the doctrine of the Trinity. But there is no salvation unless Jesus is confessed to be the Second Person of the Godhead in flesh.

   *   Faith in Christ is strictly a *personal* test. A person cannot confess Jesus as Savior for parents, siblings, children, or friends. People must experience the inner working of the Spirit to open their eyes to the reality of Christ as God's Son, which *always* results in confession of faith. Family members might claim that a parent, spouse, or sibling is a Christian, when that person does not claim to be such. I went to a home to talk with a man about his salvation. After explaining the Gospel, I asked, "Sherman, are you a Christian?" He said, "No." His wife who had overheard his answer said, "Yes you are." But he continued to deny it.

   *   The apostle Paul reinforced the thought of confession as the basis of salvation: "That if you confess with your mouth, 'Jesus is Lord (i.e. God),' and believe in your heart that God (i.e. Father) raised him from the dead, you will be saved" Rom.10:9. To confess literally means to "say the same thing." This confession is made at the time of water baptism. A pastor's teenage son stood in the baptismal waters and recited the Nicene Creed for his confession and then was immersed. But each day afterward the believer is to give a witness of Jesus Christ as God to those around him when opportunities arise.

   *   There was a *risk* associated with confessing Jesus as Savior among the Jews as John indicates, "Yet at the same time many even among the leaders believed in him. But because of the Pharisees they would not confess their faith for fear they would be put out of the

synagogue, for they loved praise from men more than praise from God" 12:42. This is true as well today. Many professing Christians have a silent witness in the world, while others pay the price for confessing Christ in the market place with their career or with their life.

 *   The local church is not a community service organization, (i.e. providing baptisms, wedding, funerals, food pantry, clothing, etc. for those who are not active participants). It is a group who confesses that Jesus Christ is God and meets to promote that truth in the community by worship and witness. Those who are not *active* in a local church are not true members of the Church, even if they insist that they are such. (I Jn. 2:19).

 We all have family members and friends who have dropped out of church for many years. It is inconceivable to me that a person can be a Christian without worshiping and fellowshipping with God's people on a regular basis.

7 A CONTRADICTION
Read: Mark 8:31-9:1

Narrative

 Knowing that the Jewish people would not accept him as the Messiah and usher in the Kingdom of God on earth, Jesus, for the first time, spoke about his *true* mission in the world--it is to give his life as a sacrifice for sins. This revelation was horrifying to the disciples, and Peter, as spokesman for the group, expressed opposition to the thought. This is not just a clumsy social faux pas, it revealed a major misunderstanding of what the mission of the Messiah was to be. The popular concept was that he was to reign as King in Jerusalem, but not to die as a condemned criminal. After Jesus had fed the five thousand they tried to take him by force to Jerusalem to make him King (Jn.6:15). The disciples were men of their time and believed the same. They were thinking that they would have positions of power when he claimed the throne of David.

Just as it was revealed to Peter by the Father that Jesus was the Messiah, Satan now made Peter a spokesman to deter Jesus from his true mission. No disciple would dare challenge his teacher, yet Peter did it. He was duped and did not know it; in that he was easily deceived and acted as a tool for the Devil. He was unaware that by rebuking Jesus for speaking of his death he had played into the hands of the Evil One. Think of the audacity of telling the Son of God that he doesn't know what his purpose is. His earlier commendation for rightly identifying Jesus as the Messiah seems to have made Peter over-confident. The natural human desire is to escape a life of suffering and shameful death, but Peter now spoke from Satan's perspective.

From the very beginning of Jesus' ministry, Satan opposed him. During the temptation in the wilderness he offered Jesus the kingdoms of the world if he would bow down and worship him (Mt.4:8,9). This was no idle boast for he controls all nations (I Jn.5:19). Jesus recognized in Peter's rebuke the same old enemy, with the same weapon of assault,
--to turn him aside from the cross. The Adversary took this opportunity to renew the original temptation.

We often think of Jesus as serene and peaceful and nothing upsetting him, but he was really human and this was a stumbling block set in his path. It was a real temptation and dangerous and he must not let his love for Peter blind him to the real source of this statement. Jesus recognized the malice of the Evil One, who is using Peter as his instrument. That he spoke harshly indicates that he was determined to be obedient to the Father's will. The rebuke of Jesus clearly warns Peter that he has miscalculated his own prospect as well as

23

that of his Lord, and he must prepare for the burden of the cross. This strong word must have brought Peter to his senses and would remain with him to the end of his life.

At this point Jesus revealed that those who follow him must take the *same path*--each bearing his own cross. The cross is an *instrument* of death to the world. Jesus dispelled any notion that those who follow him will receive the popular acclaim of the world. Instead of being celebrities they will find themselves rejected and scorned. A Messiah that will feed the hungry, heal the sick, and establish justice is what the world wants. The multitudes are not seeking spiritual truth to live a holy life. Notice, Jesus is not condemning immorality here-- simply all who live for self. A life of self-indulgence is more dangerous than a life of dissipation.

To deny self involves giving one's life to God. God's will takes precedence over human will. Jesus in the Garden prayed, "Not my will, but thy will be done." The will of God and human will are set in opposition; that is *our* cross. It can be a great or a small matter and the sacrifice may not be compared with the compensation, but when the sacrifice is great, it is still worth making it. Jesus said, "What good is it for a man to gain the whole world, yet forfeit his soul." One might lie, cheat and steal to get ahead materially, but to do so is to miss the joy of honest living. It is better to suffer the loss of all things for Christ than to lose one's eternal soul.

Application
  * The fact that Jesus began his ministry by preaching that the "kingdom of heaven is at hand" and *changing it* to "the Son of Man must suffer...be killed...and rise again" is not to go to Plan B due to the failure of Plan A. Jesus was "The Lamb of God who takes away the sin of the world!" Jn.1:29 from the very beginning. The offer of the kingdom to the Jews was

genuine, but they rejected it. This makes them responsible. It was always God's plan for his only Son to give his life as an atonement for sin (Heb.10:5-7). If the Jewish people had accepted him as the Messiah then he would have established the kingdom and they would have gone out into all the world evangelizing like the apostles did. By the means of Christ's death, however, the Gentiles will receive salvation; that was the *mystery* revealed (Eph.3:2-6).

* We too have been unconsciously used by the Devil to speak or act contrary to the purpose of God. Few of us are so spiritual all the time so as to be in agreement with what God is desiring and doing. Only a fellow Christian whose mind is saturated with Scripture can detect when what we are saying is not in agreement with God's will (I Cor.2:15,16). We then can accept their correction or resist it and persist in our error.

Are we as blind to Satan's deception as was Peter? At the end of his life, he told fellow believers: "Be self-controlled and alert. Your enemy the devil prowls around like a roaring lion looking for someone to devour. Resist him, standing firm in the faith..." I Pet.5:8,9a. He had learned this lesson the hard way and had never forgotten it. We must be constantly aware of what we say and do lest Satan use us to advance his cause.

8 AN INTERRUPTION
Read: Mark 9:2-13

Narrative
A week had passed since Jesus announced his coming death and resurrection, and the fact that all who follow him will have the *same experience*. We are not

told what conversations happened among the disciples, but there was probably much heart searching. We are told that they pondered what "rising from the dead meant" vs.10. Jesus then took Peter, James and John up Mt. Hermon (10,000 feet and snow capped) for an intense spiritual retreat. Luke tells us that Jesus went up the mountain to pray, and while doing so he was *transfigured*. The transfiguration probably took place at night so that the brilliance was magnified. The disciples had grown weary after climbing the mountain, so they dropped off to sleep, but were suddenly awakened by the light. Peter's effusive personality once again showed itself.

How did the disciples know that it was Moses and Elijah? Simple, Jesus either addressed them by name or by the subject matter. Peter was aware that during the Exodus Israel worshipped God at the Tabernacle, so he thought he was making a great suggestion that three tabernacles be built for Moses, Elijah, and Jesus. He was so excited about seeing the King in his glory that he impulsively began to speak nonsense just to say something. The narrative indicates that Moses and Elijah broke off the conversation and left because of Peter's interruption.

In speaking of building three tabernacles Peter has lowered Christ to the level of Moses and Elijah, i.e. "one of the prophets." These two men represented the Law and the Prophets that was regarded as the foundations of Jewish religion. At the death of Christ, which they were conversing about, their ministries would be fulfilled. Their glory does not compare with the glory to be revealed in Christ. To show how ridiculous is Peter's suggestion, God the Father broke in to silence him by declaring, "This is my Son, listen to him."

Application

   * The *significance* of this story is that it prepared these three disciples to endure the scandal of the cross, and it revealed Jesus as a new Moses. Even though Jesus told the disciples on three additional occasions that he would be crucified and rise again, they could not comprehend it. And, just as Moses went up on Mt.Sinai to receive the Law, Jesus was on Mt. Hermon so that the Father could declare his Sonship to these core disciples. The face of Moses became radiant as he spoke with God (Ex.32-34). Jesus also became radiant as he prayed, revealing the future glory that he would experience once he was crucified and raised to new life.

   This experience gave these three disciples hard evidence that Jesus was God. John later wrote: "The Word became flesh and made his dwelling (tabernacle) among us. We have seen his glory, the glory of the One and Only, who came from the Father, full of grace and truth" Jn.1:14. Also, at the end of his life, Peter said it did just that: "We did not follow cleverly invented stories when we told you about the power and coming of our Lord Jesus Christ, but we were eyewitnesses of his majesty. For he received honor and glory from God the Father when the voice came to him from the Majestic Glory, saying, 'This is my Son, whom I love; with him I am well pleased.' We ourselves heard this voice that came from heaven when we were with him on the sacred mountain" 2 Pet.1:16-18. The lowly condition in which Jesus Christ appeared among humanity was a continual earthly transfiguration downward; whereas this transfiguration on the mount showed the real splendor of his glory and was the essence of his natural condition (Jn.17:5). The incarnation was a veil over his
God-ness that burst forth through his flesh for these disciples to witness. That was the true Christ.

* Jesus, taking only these three disciples to the mountaintop, has been *spiritualized* by pastors to teach the victorious Christian life. The idea is that those Christians who demonstrate a greater commitment will be taken to a higher level of understanding about the life of Christ. If such persons are faithful in worship, Bible reading, prayer, and have a disciplined life, they will experience deeper spiritual insights. This is referred to as a "mountain top experience." It is true that most Christians are content to go to church occasionally and live a fairly moral life, but have no desire to spend time studying the Bible to grow in knowledge of who God is and his ways in their lives. Faithful pastors are constantly urging their people to grow to spiritual maturity. To spiritualize this passage makes for good preaching, but can produce guilt to motivate those who hear it. True spiritual growth happens as a result of a long obedience in the same direction. The peaks and valleys in the life of an average Christian are *not* what is described in this experience of these three disciples.

* There should be moments when the Spirit fills the believer and he knows it is not just emotions. This experience of the disciples teaches us that we should be *silent* in the presence of a great spiritual event. Some people think they must comment on everything, and in doing so they ruin the sacredness of the moment. The OT proverb says, "Even a fool is thought wise if he keeps silent" Prov.17:28. It is the spiritually immature who feel compelled to blurt out something. Hear the prophet Habakkuk: "But the Lord is in his holy temple, let all the earth be silent before him" Hab.2:20. When the Spirit comes in power people do not jump over pews, they get under them and hide their faces. Peter, James and John should have bowed in worship at such a sight. So should we when the Lord reveals some great spiritual truth.

* We too can have an experience of transformation like Jesus. The apostle Paul said in alluding to Moses'

experience: "Now if the ministry that brought death, which was engraved in letters on stone, came with glory, so that the Israelites could not look steadily at the face of Moses because of its glory, fading though it was, will not the ministry of the Spirit be even more glorious?...Now the Lord is the Spirit, and where the Spirit of the Lord is, there is freedom. And we, who with unveiled faces all reflect the Lord's glory, are being transformed into his likeness with ever-increasing glory, which comes from the Lord, who is the Spirit" 2 Cor.3:12,13,17,18.

How does our transformation happen? It is by "Looking into the mirror that reflects God's glory,"(KJV) i.e. saturating one's mind with the Scriptures where the nature of God is revealed (Compare James 1:22-25). Just as these three disciples looked on the true nature of Christ and were changed by it, so too can we look into the face of God in Scripture and know him more fully. This is what transforms a person.

9 AN AFFIRMATION
Read: John 6:28-35,41,47-51,58-69

Narrative
The crowds that followed Jesus were there to be healed or fed rather than to gain spiritual understanding. It looked as if his teachings had come to nothing so He decided to winnow out the true from the false followers by presenting a "hard saying." He declared himself to be the *living bread* in contrast to the manna that God provided to Israel in the wilderness. The Jewish leaders especially understood that he was claiming to be the Messiah and became hostile. Many of his would-be disciples turned away.

Jesus then asked the Twelve, "You do not want to leave too, do you?" And just as he did earlier, Peter spoke up, "Lord, to whom shall we go? You have the words of eternal life. We believe and know that you are the Holy One of God." He was honest.

There are three parts in this affirmation that we should notice. **First,** Jesus *satisfied* the deepest spiritual needs of the Twelve. His teachings had fed their spirit and given them new life. Deep insights about God and righteousness had stirred their hearts. They had seen his miracles and the feeding of the people, but his appeal to their spiritual hunger held them enthralled. His teaching about being the living bread *sifted* the crowd so that only those remained who had spiritual tastes and wants. He had given the crowd words of life not just for this world, but for eternity, yet they did not grasp them. But while in his presence, the Twelve recognized his perfect knowledge and eternal truth.

Second, Peter was convinced that Christ *alone* had the words of eternal life. He had not read the great Greek philosophers or heard the teachers of other religions, yet he knew it was useless to seek for eternal life anywhere else. To put anyone along side of Jesus as a revealer of God, as the Savior of men, is absurd. He is not just superior to all other humans, he is one of a kind. He does not require that people accept his teachings along side the teachings of other great men, or that a person hear his teachings and then go out and try to live them; no, he requires that a person make a *connection* to him (eat his flesh and drink his blood, vss.52-58). Those who reject Jesus must fashion their own gods, and many do. The alternative, as Peter saw it, was Christ or nothing.

Third, Peter states that the Twelve will remain loyal to Christ because they have seen the *essence of his nature--holiness*. More than his great teachings and wonderful miracles, these disciples had seen the personal holiness and were convinced that he was the Son of God. They had seen him in every possible circumstance and he consistently revealed the holy nature of God. Peter declared that the Twelve might not know everything and doubt much, but they are sure of this one thing: Jesus was not the sign or evidence of the thing, but was God himself present. Holiness is unique to God and they had seen it in Jesus in their day-to-day walk. When these men saw the multitudes abandon their Lord, they stood firm on the conviction because they experienced his consecrated life.

Application

  * What does the Lord require of his followers? Does he expect us to hold to certain doctrines that we might come to doubt later, or to acknowledge facts that are beyond our understanding? No. He asks only that we *obey* as much as we know from him. The teaching might be "hard," but we must wrestle with it and attempt to put it into practice. That is the way we become like him.

  *   When a conflict arises over Christ's or the apostles' teachings, it forces us to make up our *own mind* and form our personal convictions about them.

While in seminary I pastored a small, store-front church in the French Quarter of New Orleans. I decided to preach through the book of Romans, and all went well until I came to the doctrine of election and predestination in chapters 9 thru 11. Several families in the church became upset and voiced it to others, but not to me. I noticed that they had not attended for several Sundays and asked about them. I was told that they decided not to return because of my teaching on these doctrines. All I had done was explain what Paul had written. It hurt me to see them turn away from God's word.

After graduation from seminary I went to a First Church in a small town in southeast Missouri. I decided to preach through Romans again, since it contains the most basic doctrines of Christianity. This time I skipped over chapters 9 thru 11 because I thought the people might not be ready to accept these concepts. When I began to explain chapter 14 where Paul discusses the difference between strong and weak believers, many members became upset. I had unknowingly walked into a bastion of legalists. They had been taught for years that the Christian life is practiced by "don't do this and don't do that." They thought that the strong believer was the one who had stronger convictions about what a Christian *should not* do, and the weak believer was one who participated in worldly activities. When I explained that it was the opposite, and gave practical examples, some of the deacons went on a campaign to remove me. They knew nothing about "walking in the Spirit" as the only way to live as a Christian. I withstood the vote, but my ministry there was ruined. Again, I had gotten into trouble by simply explaining what Paul meant.

    * I have noticed that intense preaching of the word will sift out many who want milk rather than meat. Every church I have pastored declined in membership because I gave them the pure word Sunday-after-Sunday. Eventually everyone was offended by something I preached, just as the crowds were that heard Jesus. Of course, I hoped that the offense is the Truth taught rather than how I presented it. Over a period of years, the congregation tends to become the length and shadow of the pastor, which is a sobering thought.

    * This account should cause each believer to ask himself, "What would cause me to no longer follow Christ?" I have seen professed Christians drop by the wayside over the most trivial of matters, as well as those who quit because no one could give them answers to their questions. Seventy percent of young people who go away to university leave Christianity, and only about thirty-five percent of them will come back to it after they are into their career and married.

They succumb to skeptical professors and the party scene. But many who have been reared in church simply become bored by hearing the same shallow sermons with a different title. Shame on pastors who do not make the word of God come alive and church members who have grown weary of living under legalism. The truths of God's word are inexhaustible and we should find the Christian life exciting.

* It is still true that Jesus Christ is unique among religious teachers because he is God in flesh. Many have come on the scene, Buddha, Confucius, Mohammed, but none of them compare to the life and teachings of Jesus. He alone truly has the words of eternal life. Besides, the other founders of a world religion are all still dead and we need someone who can assure us by his own resurrection that we can live forever if we follow him. Why would anyone settle for anything less than being a disciple of Jesus? The Christian life is different from being religious because Jesus indwells every believer by the Holy Spirit.

10 A FALSE ASSUMPTION
Read: Matthew 17:24-27

Narrative

Jewish authorities in Galilee asked Peter if Jesus paid the Temple Tax. He answered, "Yes." He acted presumptuously because he didn't know for sure. His motive, no doubt, was to defend his Master. In reality, Jesus had not paid the Temple Tax and did not think it necessary. Apparently, Jesus knew of this encounter because he later asked Peter if they should pay it. There is a background to this situation that we must understand to grasp the significance of what happened next.

Under the Mosaic Law every Jewish man had to pay a Temple tax of half shekel (Ex.30:11-16). It was a reminder that God had taken the lives of first-born Egyptians during the Exodus and had spared the Jewish males. Also, it was for the maintenance of the Temple and support of the priests.

Several times during the conflict of the northern and southern kingdoms the people did not pay the tax and the Temple fell into disrepair and the priests abandoned their ministry. After the Babylonian captivity, when Nehemiah restored the Temple, the tax was reinstituted (Neh.12:44-47). However, when Nehemiah went back to Persia the people stopped paying the tax and the priests left in order to support their families (Neh.13:10,11).

When Nehemiah returned to Jerusalem he reinstituted the tax and appointed trustworthy men to oversee the distribution to the priests (Neh.13:12,13). So, there is historical precedence for paying the Temple tax.

The Jewish authorities were not genuinely concerned about Jesus' support of Temple worship. They were trying to find some religious fault in him so that they could discredit his teachings. Since this scheme did not work, they will ask later if it is right to pay taxes to Caesar, hoping to trap him (Mt.22:15-22).

We must know the circumstances to understand why they were testing him about paying taxes to Rome. When Rome conquered a country, the Senate governed it through a Proconsul (diplomat). If the country was rebellious, as was Israel, the Senate turned it over to the Emperor who sent a Procurator (military governor). Caesar was governing Israel and the troops that were sent to occupy Israel were paid for by the taxes that were raised among the Jews. In 6 A.D. a Jew in Galilee by the name of Judas (not Iscariot) had declared that anyone who used a Roman coin to pay taxes was a traitor to Judaism. He led a rebellion that Rome put down, killing him. When Jesus asked for a coin, it is amazing that someone in the crowd had one with Caesar's image on it. Jesus' wisdom is evident in the way he answered: "It is Caesar's coin and rightfully his, so give it back." His critics had no reply.

Jesus asked Peter a question, "From whom do the Kings of the earth collect taxes--from their own sons or from others?" "From others," Peter answered. "Then the sons are exempt," Jesus said. Since the Temple was the house of his Father, Jesus was not obligated to pay the Temple tax. (This also became an issue for the those who were followers of Jesus.)

Jesus had cleared the Temple at the beginning of his ministry and would clear it again during Passion Week because it had become a corrupt religious system. He is instituting a New Covenant and will be the sacrifice to put it into effect. There will be no more animal sacrifices or priesthood after his death and resurrection. So, why support it by paying the tax? This set a precedent for Jewish Christians in the Jerusalem church. They no longer needed to be part of the Temple requirements. It, of course, became a moot point after the destruction of the Temple in 70 A.D. by the Romans.

At this point Jesus did something strange: he said that he would pay the tax so as not to offend the Jews. He, no doubt, still hoped to reach some with his message. But to demonstrate to Peter that he is the Lord of Creation, he told him to go to the lake and do some bait casting to catch a fish; there he would find a coin in its mouth, making it possible to pay both their taxes. Peter did so and it happened, proving that Jesus knows all things and is sovereign of even the fish that swim in the sea (there are 24 species of fish in Galilee, most of which are caught by nets).

This is a strange story and I would not believe it unless I knew it was true. Not that fishermen have never found money in a fish's stomach, for they have, but because it was a particular fish and exactly the right coin, that makes this a miracle. This, as well as other miracles, serve to convince Peter and the other disciples that Jesus is truly God.

Application

* This statement about Caesar's image also implies that since we as humans have the impression of God's spiritual and moral image on us and that we should give ourselves back to him. We have no right to do it our way. We are not our own, we are His.

* It is essential for young pastors to be aware that they will face criticism in ministry. Many men leave seminary thinking that people are eager to hear in-depth preaching of Scripture and will love them for it. They fail to realize that when people are confronted about their failure to obey the Word that they will find fault with the pastor. It usually is not about some major point of theology; it is over whether he is loyal to some fine point of the denomination or their cultural expectations of what a pastor should be or do. They find it easier to criticize some trivial matter that is irrelevant to Scripture than to face the reality of need for change in themselves. Jesus was not naïve about the intentions of those who heard him, and neither should pastors be.

* We too should be concerned about not giving needless offense. The apostle Paul explained this principle in I Cor.9:19-23. In non-moral matters a Christian can bend in order to win others to Christ. Paul said that he adapted himself to Jews (Acts 21:17-26), Gentiles, and persons of overly scrupulous conscience (i.e. weak), "so that by all means he might save some." In other words, some things do not matter and are not worth going to the wall for. We must, however, have discernment about what is primary and what is of secondary importance. For example, Paul refused to bend over the issue of Gentiles being circumcised to become Christians because it was a matter of salvation being by grace through faith alone (Acts 15:5; Gal.5:2-6). However, a secondary matter about whether to eat

36

food offered to an idol and which day to gather for worship, he allowed Christians to differ (Rom.14:2-5, 13-22).

11 FORGIVING OTHERS
Read: Matthew 18:21, 22

Narrative

The disciples were together constantly over a year and a half. Surely there were conflicts among them. We know they were jealous of one another and bickered among themselves (Mk.9:33,34; Mt.20:20,21,24)). Such happenings probably prompted Peter to ask about forgiveness. The Rabbis taught that one should forgive an offender three times.
Peter thought he was being generous by asking if seven times was enough. Jesus used an exorbitant number to say that God's people ought not carry resentment. An offense should be faced and resolved as soon as possible.

We are familiar with Jesus' teachings about forgiveness, but let us briefly review them.
First, if a Christian has sinned against someone he should make it right before he comes to worship (Mt.5:23,24).
Second, if a Christian is sinned against by a fellow believer, he should go to that offender and point out the problem and expect an apology (Mt.18:15ff). The object of this teaching is *unity of spirit* in the church. If the offender will not acknowledge his sin, he is to be regarded as an outsider by the church. We have no

37

account of Jesus forgiving his enemies. Why?

Application

*   Most of us have known people in the past, maybe even counted them as friends, whom we no longer have a relationship with. It might be due to the changes that have taken place in both of us, or we felt betrayed by something the person said or did. It is common for Christians to feel guilty that they have not forgiven everyone that wronged them. We need to realize that we are *not required* to have a relationship with those who offend us.

The prophet Amos asked a key question regarding *relationships*: "Do two walk together unless they agree to do so?" (3:3). The answer is, of course not; they cannot and it is hypocritical to pretend to do so.

The Psalmist said about relationships: "How good and pleasant it is when brothers live together in unity!" Ps.133:1. The reality is that it is unusual to maintain a friendship over a long period of time because they see one another too much and it turns sour, or they do not see one another often enough and they drift apart. It is inevitable that offenses will arise, and if they are not forgiven, the relationship cannot continue. David said, "If an enemy were insulting me, I could endure it; if a foe were raising himself against me, I could hide from him. But it is you, a man like myself, my companion, my close friend, with whom I once enjoyed sweet fellowship as we walked with the throng at the house of God...My companion attacks his friends; he violates his covenant. His speech is smooth as butter, yet war is in his heart; his words are more soothing than oil, yet they are drawn swords" Ps.55:12-14,20,21. It is one thing for a neighbor, or a fellow worker, of even a family member to say or do hurtful things, but the worst of all is a brother or sister in the Lord with whom we have worshipped who turns against us and becomes an enemy.

* The story that Jesus told (vss.23-35) to illustrate forgiving others an *unlimited amount* of offenses perfectly explains the statement in the Lord's prayer: "Forgive us our debts as we forgive our debtors." A King forgave his servant an impossible debt to pay, but the servant went out and did not forgive a fellow servant that owed an average debt. This points out that as sinners it was impossible for us to pay our sin debt, so God forgave us when we repented. Because we have been forgiven an extreme debt, surely, we can forgive others who come and ask our forgiveness. If we find no place for forgiveness *from the heart* (not just with the lips), it indicates that we have not experienced God's forgiveness. When we have truly forgiven the offender, who has confessed his wrong, we are able to wish the person well in life.

The apostle Paul urged believers "to get rid of all bitterness, rage and anger, brawling and slander, along with every form of malice. Be kind and compassionate to one another, forgiving each other, just as in Christ God forgave you" Eph.4:31,32. It should be expected that those who receive the forgiveness that God offers in the gospel would display something of their character and show a forgiving attitude to others. If we do not have a forgiving spirit, can we have any assurance that God has forgiven us?

* The simple truth of why offenders are not forgiven is this: One cannot forgive an enemy who *never comes* and admits his evil intentions (Prov.18:19). David, Jesus and Paul did not forgive their enemies because they never came and asked (Lk.17:3,4;2 Tim.4:14,15). (Jesus forgave those who repented of their sins against God, as well as the soldiers that crucified him because of their ignorance. They were acting for the Roman State; it was not personal.)

There is so much *sentimentality* associated with forgiveness that this basic truth has been overlooked. Some people will never admit that they have wronged anyone. But the general opinion that the offended

39

person should just go ahead and forgive the person anyway is worse than refusing to forgive a person who comes and admits his wrong. There is a principle here that has been forgotten by this overly sensate, touchy-feely culture we live in. Others who are emotionally weak are constantly apologizing for imagined wrongs they have done. They will even ask, "If I have offended you, please forgive me," when they should wait for the person they supposedly offended to come to them.

If a Christian wants to have a relationship with the offender, he must go to that person and point out the offense. The offended person might or might not admit his wrong and ask forgiveness. Of course, we must forgive such a person if he does admit his wrong (70 times 7). But if there is no desire to continue a relationship with the offender, we should move on by making other friends.

To sum it up, the *axiom* laid down by the writer of Proverbs seems good: "He who covers over an offense promotes love, but whoever repeats the matter separates close friends" 17:9. Some things should never be repeated if a relationship is to continue. The apostle Paul also gives wise counsel: "If it is possible, as far as it depends on you, live in peace with everyone" Rom.12:18. Some people are impossible to get along with. They are so difficult that to have a relationship with them one must become emotionally unstable. People who are bitter and angry should be avoided because it is only a matter of time before you become the object of their wrath.

12 A COMPLAINT
Read: Mark 10:17-31

Narrative

Jesus was asked by a young man, "what good thing must I do to inherit eternal life?" His fallacy was that he assumed salvation was by doing good works, so Jesus showed him that it is not a matter of goodness. When he told the man to "keep the commandments," Jesus knew that he thought he had obeyed them; when in reality he had not. To show the rich man was guilty of breaking the tenth commandment (covetousness), Jesus told him to "sell his possessions and give the money to the poor." As he walked away, Jesus made a comment to the disciples, "How hard it is for the rich to enter the kingdom of God!" Then he used the proverbial phrase, common in use at that time, of how "impossible for a camel to go through the eye of a needle." He did so to highlight the truth that salvation is not possible for those who set their heart on riches. It is not the riches themselves, but their *trust* in riches that is condemned by Jesus.

The disciples probably thought that by following Jesus they would be exalted when Jesus came to rule his kingdom. Now, two years later, they have nothing to show for their obedience except sleeping on the ground, walking dusty roads, wearing dirty clothes, eating whatever was given them, fighting off the crowds. The impulsive disciple, Simon Peter, so much given to think aloud, blurted out an honest complaint: "We have left everything to follow you! What then will there be for us?" (Mt.19:27). To paraphrase it: "We have made a sacrifice and what compensation will we receive?"

At the beginning, when Jesus called the disciples to follow him, he did not promise them any compensation. They had learned that not riches and power, but hardship and suffering came as a result of being his disciple. Indeed, they had denied themselves and taken up his cross. It must have come to mind as they heard Jesus interacting with the rich man, "What good will it be for a man if he gains the whole world, yet forfeits his soul? Or what can a man give in exchange for his soul?" Mk.8:36. Now, however, the question naturally arose, "What will be our reward for leaving everything?"

The belief of the Jews at this time was that if a person were obedient to the Law the Lord would bless him *materially*. In brief, riches were evidence of God's approval (e.g. Abraham, Gen.24:34,35), so said the OT.

Jesus made a promise that his disciples would be rewarded for their sacrifice, but *not in this life*: "When I come in glory to establish my kingdom on earth you will reign with me over Israel and receive a hundred times as many riches" (Mt.19:28). Notice, he is very specific about when the disciples will be rewarded, which means that this cannot be a general principle. This interpretation must be true because none of the disciples were wealthy in material goods, but they were rich in having a spiritual family with all its resources. The rewards for obedience to Christ during the church age are *spiritual* rather than material. This is evident among Christians the world over.

Application
    * Does it pay to serve God? Some of the Jewish believers during the prophet Malachi's time wondered if it was worth serving God (Mal.3:13-18). They are assured that at the end time a distinction will be made between those who served God and those who did not. Television evangelists that preach material possessions will come in this life if one serves the Lord are deceiving those who believe them. He might become wealthy because he has fleeced the Lord's sheep, but the believers who give will be disappointed in the Lord because they have not reaped a hundred-fold increase from their sacrificial giving. One must choose to follow Christ for his own sake, not for what material gains he

might receive. Many believers around the world have suffered the loss of everything, and some family members killed because of Christ. The writer of Hebrews said, "And without faith it is impossible to please God, because anyone who comes to him must believe that he exists and that he rewards those who earnestly seek him" 11:6. These rewards are spiritual, not material possessions.

  * What kind of good works bring reward? Depending on their *motivation* for doing good works, believers either gain rewards or lose them. Believers can produce works of wood, hay and stubble, or gold, silver and precious stones (I Cor.3:11-15). The former works will be burned up because they are for *self-glorification* while the latter works *glorify the Lord* and will be purified into crowns that believers will cast at his feet. For example: my wife is a church pianist who practices for hours to present something of excellence to the Lord in Sunday worship, whereas, a concert pianist also practices for weeks to play a great composition for the pleasure of the audience will be applauded. What is the difference? My wife does it for the glory of God but the concert pianist does it to receive glory for self. Sadly, many pastors are busy building their own kingdom by exalting themselves rather than building the kingdom of God by focusing on Christ. They will suffer loss at the Judgment.

  * What is the *normal* Christian life? Many of us feel guilty when we hear of people who have left secular jobs, family relationships, houses and cars, to serve Christ sacrificially in some distant land. It should be obvious what would happen if every Christian left these things to follow Christ. Who would support the local ministry of the church? How many wealthy people did it take to keep the disciples poor? When the disciples left their means of earning a living, someone had to support them and their families. Christ does not demand that every Christian go as a missionary into all the world else who would support them? Some have to

stay at home and earn enough to give. The vast majority of us simply need to be *faithful* to Christ where we are: such as, getting married and raising a godly family, being a reliable employee, contributing to the community, playing sports, recreating, vacationing, serving in a local church, supporting its ministries, and witnessing of Christ to those we meet along the way. Remember, the demon possessed man wanted to follow Jesus after he was healed, but Jesus said, "Go home to your family and tell them how much the Lord has done for you, and how he has had mercy on you" Mk.5:18-20. That is all he requires for most of us, and we should be content in it. We do not need to be a wild-eyed fanatic to be fully committed to Christ; we only need to be faithful in service where we are.

13 THEOLOGICAL CURIOSITY
Read: Mark 11:12-24

Narrative

The crowd had no sooner declared that Jesus is the Messiah than he performed an act of *judgment* by clearing the Temple, and then illustrated it with an object lesson of cursing the fig tree. It was a dramatized *act of prophecy* for the instruction of his disciples. Peter inquired about the connection of clearing the Temple and cursing of the fig tree. This curiosity is one of Simon Peter's good traits.

On Monday morning of Passion Week, as Jesus went from Bethany to Jerusalem, he was hungry and stopped to gather figs from a tree. The fig tree was full

44

of leaves, but there were no buds. It was two months before ripe figs would be on the tree, but there should be indications that it would be fruitful. Because there wasn't, so Jesus cursed it and passed on.

Should a tree, not being a moral agent, be punished for its condition? He judged the tree, not because of its lack of figs, but because it *pretended* with many leaves to be a fruitful tree. As a symbol of the Jewish nation it pointed to their spiritual condition. The Temple and the priestly system of worship was leafy (ostentatious) but offered no true salvation.

Surely the disciples remembered the story of the barren fig tree in the vineyard (Lk.13:6-9). The startling thing about Jesus' cursing the fig tree is that its leaves withered by the next day (Tuesday). Peter was perceptive enough to associate the clearing of the Temple with the sudden withering of the fig tree as signs of judgment on Israel.

The fig tree was a symbol both of Israel's *prosperity* (1 Kgs.4:25; Micah 4:4; Zech.3:10) as well as its *destruction* (Jer.5:17; Hosea 2:12; Joel 1:7,12). Instead of bearing the fruit of salvation, Jewish religion was all show and no substance. The Jews, with their revelation of God, were supposed to evangelize the nations, but they had failed because their religion had become exclusive—Jews only.

His act of clearing the Temple and cursing the fig tree was a *prophecy* that the Lord would soon judge the Jewish nation for their refusal to accept the offer of the Messianic kingdom through his Son, Christ Jesus. The triumphal entry was to be the coronation of Jesus, but it turned into his crucifixion. As a result of this, judgment happened within one generation (70 A.D.).

Jesus also used the cursing of the barren fig tree as a example of the power of faith. Faith is "able to move mountains." In a figurative sense, the greatest possible difficulties can be removed when a person has faith (James 1:6). Prayer is the source of power of such faith. A strong faith is dependent on God's power.

45

Application

   * On several occasions Jesus was exasperated with the disciples because they did not comprehend what he was teaching. They were theologically slow. Not just because they lacked formal education, but because they were not spiritually aware. But on this occasion, Peter was inquisitive enough to ask a question. He connected Jesus' clearing of the Temple with the withering of the fig tree and the symbolism of judgment to come.

   Most of us are not *theologically* minded. We seem content to know the Bible stories and listen to the pastor retell them. Theology is a level beyond just knowing the Bible; it is arranging the teachings of Scripture *systematically* so that apparent contradictions are resolved. This process makes the believer strong enough to overcome doubts. People in the cults appear to know the Bible well, but when they are questioned, it becomes obvious that they have learned some of the Scriptures and ignored the others that do not fit their scheme. God cannot contradict himself, so there ought to be a unity in Scripture. We should be able to connect all the dots to get a full picture of who God is and what he is about in the world.

   * Another truth related to this story is: God is *not finished* with the Jewish people, even though they were scattered by the destruction of Jerusalem in 70 and 134 A.D. The OT prophets stated that the Jews will return to the land of Abraham just before the return of Christ. The present state of Israel might *not* be a fulfillment of these prophesies because it is a political entity and not a spiritual one. It could be invaded and destroyed by its surrounding Muslim enemies. However, the apostle Paul stated that the Lord will "save all Israel" at some point in the future (Rom.11:25-32). There are many OT prophecies about Israel that were not fulfilled in Christ's first coming.

   * All of this seems too *literal* for liberal pastors and professors. Their complaint is that it is too speculative. Many of them believe the "key" to prophecy has been lost, which relieves them of having to study it in order to preach it to their congregations. Yet, the book of Revelation promises a blessing to those who read its prophecies. Some preaching on prophecy is more science fiction than reality and should be ignored. But, we need to understand prophecy in order to have hope about the future. That was the purpose Jesus gave it.

14 WHEN AND WHAT?
Read: Mark 13:1-4

Narrative

During Passion Week as Jesus was in the Temple preaching, the disciples commented on its splendor. It was begun by King Herod forty-six years earlier. In the midst of this discussion Jesus prophesied that the Temple would be destroyed. After they left the city they stopped on the Mount of Olives and looked back on the Temple. Peter, Andrew, James and John then asked *when* these things would happen and *what* would be the signs. As we read further, we realize that Jesus did not answer *when*, but he described *what* would happen.

It is broken down into what would happen in their lifetime as well as what would happen at the End time. Verses 3-13,28-31 happened in 70 A.D, while verses 14-27, 32-37 will happen at his Second Coming. The signs, therefore, are for the disciples' generation and the generation living when the Anti-Christ appears (2 Thess. 2:1-4).

We should not concern ourselves with when because no one really knows (vss.32-37). A believer should not panic or be alarmed if a preacher predicts when Christ will return because it is in the Father's mind alone. All the date setters are eventually embarrassed.

Even after this teaching the disciples were still concerned about *when* Jesus would come again. At the Mount of Olives, just before he ascended, the disciples asked, "Lord, are you at this time going to restore the kingdom to Israel?" (Acts 1:6). They were *obsessed* with when Last Things would happen. Jesus answered, "It is not for you to know the times or dates the Father has set by his own authority" (vs.7). They learned, however, that the Lord has another kingdom that will soon come (i.e. the Church).

Application

* One of the first serious studies of Scripture I made as a young preacher was Last Things. The Second Coming of Christ was an intriguing subject with so many facets that I spent several years digging into it. I read all the books by the popular preachers. Every opportunity to preach I spoke on what would happen in the future. I believed the return of Christ would happen in my lifetime, which added conviction to my preaching. People seemed to like the sermons so I was encouraged to dwell on the subject. I drew time-line charts to help them understand. My ministry was focused on prophecy for my first three or four years. I have used this material on-and-off in every church since. But I noticed that people did not change their way of living as a result of this teaching. It was fascinating to them, but did not impact their attitudes or behavior. My emphasis changed forty years ago to a study of how to live the Christian life. This has proved to be more effective in changing lives.

* There is a generation that will experience the Second Coming of Christ (I Thess. 4:13-18), but for most of us the second coming of Christ will happen at the moment of death. Therefore, the stress should be on living the Christian life. The apostle Peter stopped

speculating about when Christ would return and concentrated on teaching others how to live the life of Christ daily (2 Pet.3:3,8-13). This was also the emphasis of the apostle Paul (Rom.13:11-14).

15 BECOMING A SERVANT
Read: John 13:1-17

Narrative

On the last evening of his life (Wednesday at 6 pm), Jesus and the disciples gathered in an Upper Room to observe a pre-Passover meal. According to John, Jesus was crucified on Thursday, the day of Preparation for Passover, rather than Friday as traditionally held.

As the disciples entered the room they reclined at a low table, with their feet protruding outward. A pitcher of water, a basin and a towel were on a table by the door, but none of them noticed. Normally a servant washed the feet of the guest, but no servant was present. The roads were dusty, and since most people wore sandals, their feet became hot and dirty. To have cool water poured over one's feet and wiped with a towel was refreshing.

None of the disciples were willing to play the role of a servant because they had been arguing about who was the greatest and would have the place of honor at the meal. Luke records, "Also a dispute arose among them as to which of them was considered to be greatest..." Jesus said, "...the greatest among you should be like the youngest, and the one who rules like the one who serves. For who is greater, the one who is at the table or the one who serves? Is it not the one who is at the table? But I am among you as one who serves" Lk.22:24,26,27. For anyone of them to wash the feet of the others was to declare himself a servant of all, and that is precisely what each one determined not to do. No one who is insecure will humble himself to serve another.

How was Jesus to awaken them to humility and love for one another? An object lesson that they would never forget was in order. He got up from the table and gird himself with a towel, took the water pitcher and basin and knelt by the feet of the first disciple. The room fell silent with conversation as each disciple saw what Jesus was doing. Did they feel bitter humiliation and burning shame that their Lord would do what anyone of them should have done?

John the apostle commented on the mood of Jesus. This was the final hours and Jesus knew what lay ahead: betrayal by Judas, desertion by the disciples, unjust trials and torture, and the pain of death, but most of all, to be the sin bearer for humanity. Yet, he was focused on showing the disciples what love meant. These jealous and childish men witnessed the sacrificial love of Jesus.

How could Jesus humble himself so? He was *fully conscious of who he was* and was not threatened by washing the disciples' feet. Jesus took the disguise of a household servant. Here is an illustration of the greater truth of the incarnation! Jesus was not insecure or full of pride, so he could humble himself and serve the disciples.

Shame and astonishment shut the mouths of the disciples as Jesus washed the feet of each one, until he came to Peter. To his credit he refused because he knew the situation should be reversed. Jesus answered his objection by saying that an explanation would come forth later. But this did not satisfy Peter. Out came one of his blunt and hasty comments, "No, you will never wash my feet." Self-confident, Peter once again crossed a line. The first requirement of a disciple is self-surrender. His first refusal was overlooked as a reaction, but the second is an obstinate, proud, a self-righteous utterance, and was quickly met by Jesus rebuke: "Unless I wash you, you have no part with me." Peter protested the washing because he recognized the absurdity of the situation. He should be washing the feet of Jesus. Unless he was prepared to leave the room and reckon himself as an outcast from the company, he must submit to this ritual like the other disciples. So, he gave the typical response by going to the other extreme and offered his hands and head to be washed. Here again Peter was swayed by blind impulse, and erred. If he could only hold his tongue instead of reacting! What shame must have swept over him. Jesus then pointed out that the daily use of the bath rendered it needless to wash more than feet. The disciples, except Judas, had been spiritually cleansed and only needed refreshing. Thus, Jesus made a distinction between *present defilement* and *habitual impurity*. This act symbolized the cleansing of their proud feelings that had built up over three years. Was there one of them that was not broken down by this act of the Lord Jesus?

Jesus was not content to let his actions speak for themselves; he expressly explained the meaning of what he had done (vss.12-17). He meant that they should learn to be humble and be ready to serve one another. He did not, however, establish it as an ordinance or sacrament for the Church to observe because we fulfill it when we show humility in a hundred different ways. (We do not wear sandals or travel on dusty roads.)

Application
* A servant spirit is *not natural*, but it can be developed. Simon Peter learned this lesson for in later life he wrote: "All of you live in harmony with one another; be sympathetic, love as brothers, be compassionate and humble" I Pet.3:8. Some pastors find it hard to be humble. Much like the Pharisees, they like to have a place of honor and be recognized

(Mt.23:5-12). Here the principle of becoming a servant was laid down: "Whoever exalts himself will be humbled, and whoever humbles himself will be exalted."

I once served as associate pastor of a mid-size church and one of my responsibilities was the Wednesday night dinners. Before going to the various classes offered, people gathered in the fellowship hall for a meal. I organized it so that a different Sunday School class would serve in the cafeteria line. In one staff meeting I suggested to the seven pastors that we all take a turn at serving for a month. The only one to hesitate was the senior pastor. He thought it would affect his dignity before the people. He regarded the church as a corporation and himself as the Chief Executive Officer with the associate pastors as Chief Operating Officers and the church members as employees. He was so elitist that only white-collar professionals were considered to serve as elders. It also was beneath him to mix with the little people at social functions. I thought pastors were to be servants and expressed it in that staff meeting. Finally, all the associate pastors agreed and I set the date. As the people came through the line that night many of them expressed surprise and amazement that the pastors would put on an apron to serve food and then clear the tables. When the senior pastor saw the impact of servanthood by the associates he then volunteered. Not only do pastors need to learn to be servants, so do many pretentious members. We must do the small services that each hour calls for, to follow Jesus who girt himself with the slave's apron. As often as we do so we are being like him.

    * Church members who seldom attend need to consider the statement of Jesus to Peter that if he did not participate in the foot washing, he had no part with Christ. Even though foot washing is not an ordinance or

sacrament of the church, the ordinances of baptism and the Lord's Supper are *essential* to identification with Christ, so that I can absolutely say that any person who has not been baptized and does not regularly participate in holy communion has "no part with Christ." Most of us have family members and friends who hold church membership, but attend only for special events. I fear for their salvation because they think that all is well, when in reality they are not taking part in Christ.

  * Another great truth in this passage is: Even though genuine believers' sin occasionally, they do not need regeneration again; they only need to confess the sin and be restored to fellowship with Christ (Heb.6:4-6). Our *relationship* with Christ (justification, adoption, regeneration, etc.) cannot be broken by any number of sins or their severity, but our *fellowship* (prayer, joy, peace, etc.) with him can be. Our heart has been cleansed from sin, but by just walking through a sinful world as we must do, our feet become dirty. Only by admitting that we need our souls washed, and by humbly allowing the Spirit to wash them, are we brought back into fellowship with Christ.

16   A FOOLISH BOAST
Read: Mark 14:27-31

Narrative
  The first surprise Jesus dropped on the disciples in the Upper Room was that one of them would *betray*

him. They wondered who it could be? Jesus identified the betrayer as the one who dipped his bread in the sauce at the same time he did. John and Peter then recognized Judas as the one.

The next surprise came when they left the Upper Room around midnight to make their way to Gethsemane. While walking through the city, Jesus revealed that all the disciples would *desert* him before the night was over. Peter vehemently declared: "even if all fall away, I will not." Then Jesus became specific, "Before the rooster crows twice, you will deny me three times." But Peter insisted emphatically, "Even if I have to die with you, I will never disown you." The others heard this conversation and were as confident as Peter. However, he was the loudest in his protestations, and there is a painful egotism in his boast.

In the parallel reading of John (13:33-38) Jesus had just told them that he is about to leave them and the mark of their discipleship is love for one another. Peter ignores the teaching on love and wants to know where Jesus is going. The Church is not like any other association. Most organizations are based on race, wealth, status, education, etc. Peter does not want to know how Christians show their love. Jesus noticed that none of his disciples asked him about love of one another (Jn. 16:5). Jesus tells Peter that he will deny him and that he will follow him (in death) later (Jn. 21:18,19).

The disciples felt safe because they had heard Jesus pray just a few hours before: "[Father] while I was with them, I protected them and kept them safe by that name you gave me...My prayer is not that you take them out of the world but that you protect them from the evil one" Jn.17:12,15. They ran away when Jesus was arrested, but their abandonment of him was only *temporary because he had prayed for them*.

Jesus gave a stern warning earlier about denial when he said, "Whosoever shall deny me, him will I deny before my Father in heaven" Mt.10:33. Surely the disciples had heard this statement. It is possible to deny Christ by *what is said* or *not said* to others. To curse his name is surely to deny him, but not to speak up around others to defend his name is also denial of Christ. It is also possible to deny him by *one's actions* (Titus 1:16). To claim to be a follower of Christ and exclude him from our daily decisions is a form of denial. Many think of themselves as Christians, but they practice a completely *secular* lifestyle. They are good people, but they seldom attend worship, never give anything to the church, never read the Bible or have serious prayer. This is probably the most common form of denial. Denial is a lifetime of not acknowledging Christ as God, not a temporary lapse because of some life or death circumstance such as Peter found himself in.

As Peter and John warmed themselves by the fire, a servant girl accused Peter of being a follower of Jesus (vss. 66-72). The Galilean accent gave him away. On another instance Peter even invoked curses on himself to reinforce his denial of knowing Jesus. The rooster crowed the second time (2:30 a.m.?) and he remembered what Jesus had said. He went out and wept at his cowardice.

Application

   * Simon Peter's personality is the type that lends itself to bold statements that conceal weakness. He failed because of *over confidence.* Paul gave the warning to believers at Corinth: "...if you think you are standing firm, be careful that you don't fall!" I Cor.10:12. Such a person usually makes strong claims about what he will do if..., but when the confrontation comes, he does not stand strong. This bravado is soon exposed. Peter is like the schoolyard bully who intimidates other children until one of them punches him out and the Bully runs crying to the teacher. We have seen this pattern before. The silent person is the one who often acts as a hero under pressure. In contrast, John did not deny Jesus in

the courtyard of Caiaphas or at his trial before Pilate; he was even at the crucifixion with the mother of Jesus.

* During the 250 years of Roman persecution of Christians many of them were arrested and tried for not burning incense to Caesar as god. Often they were given the chance to renounce Christ, rather than be tortured and put to death, and some of them did. After they were released, these believers returned to the church and asked to be forgiven. This caused a division in practice among some churches. Some accepted them back if they repented while others flatly refused. It was during this time that the phrase "I believe in the forgiveness of sins" was added to the Apostles' Creed.

* Like Peter, we too might think that we would never deny our Lord no matter what the circumstance. But the reality is, when facing death for our belief in him, we cannot be sure what we might do. We hope that we would not deny him. Does torture and threat of death really reveal what is in one's heart? No. I think the Lord takes into account the situation of one's denial of him because he knows what a person really believes.

* Just as Jesus prayed for the Father to keep the disciples from ultimate apostasy, he also prayed that every believer would ultimately make it to heaven (Jn.17:12,15). He taught the disciples earlier that the Father keeps safe all the sheep in his flock (Jn.10:27-30). This might have caused them to be presumptuous. After all, they did not watch and pray in the Garden, but fell into temptation. Every true believer is *secure* because he is kept in the Father's hands, but this does not mean that we are not responsible for being diligent in our Christian walk.

17 A KINGDOM BY FORCE

Read: John 18:1-11

Jesus and the disciples crossed the Kidron valley, and entered the Garden of Gethsemane, on the western slope of the Mt. of Olives. While Jesus had been observing a pre-Passover meal with the disciples, Judas was making preparations for Jesus' arrest. Judas led Temple guards and a cohort of Roman soldiers to take Jesus captive. The moon was full and almost like day, but they came with torches to make sure they found him.

Why the Roman cohort of 500 men? Perhaps Judas remembered the miraculous power of Jesus and feared that he might use it to escape.

When the accounts of the arrest in the Four Gospels are harmonized the arrest seems to have happened in the following order.

1. Judas immediately approached Jesus and gave the betrayal kiss (Mt.26:47-50). This was the signal to arrest him.

2. Jesus stepped forward and asked, "Who is it you want?" They replied, "Jesus of Nazareth." He answered, "I am he." (text)

3. Some of the Temple guards laid hands on several of the disciples to arrest them (e.g. John Mark, Mk.14:51,52), but Jesus intervened, "If you are looking for me, then let these men go" (Jn.18:8).

4. While he was resigned to his destiny because he knew it was the Father's will (vs.4a), Jesus was not without a sense of the injustice that was being done to him, therefore he said to the mob, "Am I leading a rebellion, that you have come out with swords and clubs to capture me? Everyday I sat in the temple courts teaching, and you did not arrest me?" Mk.14:48-50.

5. Some of the disciples asked him as the Temple guards approached, "Lord, should we strike with our swords?" Lk.22:49. He had told them earlier to purchase swords to defend themselves (Lk.22:36-38).

6. Peter acted to protect Jesus by taking a swing with his sword and cut off the right ear of Malchus, a servant of the High Priest. Jesus rebuked him by pointing out that this was not the time to fight because it was the Father's will that he be arrested and put to death (Jn.18:4,11). Besides, he warned, those who "live by the sword, will die by the sword."

7. Jesus then performed his last miracle of compassion by restoring the severed ear to Malchus. Why did no one recognize the miracle?

8. It is at this point that all the disciples fled the scene because the soldiers began reaching out to grab them and take them in as well. Mark fled leaving his outer cloak behind (Mk.14:51,52).

9. Peter and John, however, quickly recovered and followed the soldiers to the house of Annas and Caiaphas (vss.12-14).

Application

    * Some think that Jesus' protecting the disciples from being arrested, tried and crucified with him is proof that he will not allow any of his servants to be put to death for their witness. I have heard the testimony of Christians who lost a husband or wife express disappointment that the Lord did not deliver their loved one from danger. On the other hand, I have heard testimonies of Christians being miraculously delivered from the death. Why one and not another? All we can conclude is that the *purpose* of God for each of his servants is different. Jesus protected the disciples during his arrest because they had not yet gone out on their mission to the world. They were a special group. This cannot be said of all the servants of God who have gone out into the world in the past twenty centuries. Many have died because of their witness to Jesus Christ as Lord. There is no promise of protection from harm while on mission for Christ, there is however, a *promise*

of persecution. Jesus said that he would be with the Christian *through* persecution, but not deliver them from it (Mt.28:20). Many have experienced his presence and were able to endure the persecution and death.

* This incident also teaches us that the kingdom of God is *not to be spread by forcing people to submit to it.* No coercion is to be used in making converts (contrast with Islam). Sinners are to be persuaded by preaching the good news of sins forgiven and eternal life for all who repent and believe. In fact, Christians were forbidden by the early church to use the sword for defense even when persecuted. Tertullian (c.197) said, "We willingly yield ourselves to the sword. So what wars would we not be both fit and eager to participate in, if in our religion it were not counted better to be slain than to slay." When this message is accompanied by the convicting power of the Holy Spirit, sinners do not resist. However, those who hear the gospel can exercise their will and walk away. Many have done so.

* The Roman Church should be ashamed that it used an Inquisition to force Jews to convert to Christianity or die. Those who could, fled from such persecution, and rightly so. This practice of Roman Catholicism during the Middle Ages did not represent biblical Christianity. It was a matter of retaining political power. They also put Protestants to death for leaving the Roman Church. True Christianity doesn't compel anyone to convert.

* Muslims believe that the Roman soldiers crucified Judas instead of Jesus. They base their belief on the Gospel of Barnabas, not to be confused with the Epistle of Barnabas (c.170-190). Muslims like this *Gnostic* Gospel because it denies that Jesus was the Son of God. Scholars know that it is apocryphal because there are no early Greek manuscripts for it. None of the Church Fathers reference it in their writings. There are numerous historical errors, as well as anachronisms

from the Middle Ages. There are Islamic elements throughout which indicate that it was written in the 14th century by a European convert to Islam. By believing the Gospel of Barnabas instead of the Four Gospels Muslims cut themselves off from salvation because their knowledge of Jesus Christ is wrong. Saving faith consists of three parts: accurate *knowledge* of Christ's person and works; mental ascent that who he was and what he did is *true*; and, placing one's *trust* in this Christ. Without the crucifixion of Christ there is no atonement or resurrection, which in turn means there is no forgiveness of sins or eternal life.

   * Christians used *persuasive reasoning* to evangelize, whereas the primary means Muslims used to spread the message of Mohammed was the sword. Under Islam people were given the option to convert and become second-class citizens or be put to death. Thirty thousand churches were destroyed in the Byzantine Empire alone, and the number of Christians put to death is unknown. The advance of Islam into Persia to the east, across north Africa into Spain in the west, and north into Turkey and into the Balkans happened over a period of eight hundred years. The Crusades were a *just response* to Muslims destroying the holy places in Jerusalem. Muslims were finally stopped at the Battle of Tours (732) in France and the Battle of Lepanto (1571) outside Venice. The Ottoman Empire was broken up after WWI.

   However, a radical Islam has arisen in the last 40 years, supported by oil money, and is spreading its violence across the world. Churches are being destroyed and Christians put to death by the thousands each day. Not only do they kill Christians, they regard Jews, Buddhists, and Hindus, as infidels and kill them as well. It is the fastest growing world religion because it uses force to make converts. Even the different sects of Muslims, Sunnis and Shias, kill each other. We can only conclude that it is a *violent* religion.

It is against the law in Muslim countries to convert to Christianity. Some have done so and they have been imprisoned and/or put to death, as well as their family members. Nevertheless, these political or religious barriers are being breeched by Muslims having visions and dreams of Jesus and converting as a result. Many remain silent because of the fear of death, but some are bold and declare their faith in Christ as Savior, then flee to another country.

  * Jesus said that he brought a different kind of sword. It is *spiritual* and causes division in families and friends (Mt.10:34). An extreme example of spiritual truth separating families is Levi killing members of his family who had worshipped the golden calf (Ex.32:25-29; Deut. 33:8,9). It is the sword of the Spirit, the word of God that convicts sinners and sanctifies believers (Eph.6:17; Jn.17:17)). This sword is sharper than a physical sword because it penetrates to the inward parts of a sinner and produces regeneration (Heb.4:12). The most effective means of reaching others for Christ, is to ask them to read the Bible straight through and then answer their questions.

18 PETER BELIEVED
Read: John 20:1-9

Narrative
As we read the resurrection accounts in the Four Gospels, we should realize they must be harmonized to make sense, because they tell of different encounters with the risen Christ by various persons. The

discrepancies in the Four Gospels actually *strengthen* the eyewitness accounts because people always have a different perspective of any event.

To begin: "Why were the women going to the tomb?" The body of Jesus had to be entombed before the Passover at 6pm on Thursday. They did not have time to apply the spices to the wrappings so they were coming to complete the process (Lk.23:55,56). Motivated by their love for Jesus they overlooked two important facts: Pilate had placed the Roman seal on the tomb which was guarded by soldiers (Mt.27: 65,66). John and these women had seen it sealed, so how would they get into the tomb? Maybe the women thought they could talk the soldiers into moving the large stone. Peter had missed the crucifixion and the burial, but John had witnessed both. Now these two men missed the greatest event in human history. Was it because they were being *logical* about not going to the tomb that was sealed and guarded? Had the women asked them to join them and they dismissed it as nonsense? After all, even when Mary Magdalene told them that the tomb was empty they thought she was being hysterical (Lk.24:11).

Matthew tells us that the Roman guards fled out of fear when the earth shook and the angel rolled the stone away. From John we learn that Mary Magdalene came early to the tomb. Matthew indicates that four or five other women accompanied her. Mark states that the women brought spices to cover the odor of the decaying body; then John tells how Mary, seeing the empty tomb ran to tell Peter and John. The *greatest announcement ever made* was by a woman. At this time a woman's testimony was not accepted in a Jewish court, but God used one to be the first witness of the resurrection. She also was a woman from whom Jesus had cast out seven demons. One can imagine what evils she was guilty of. Mary, along with these other women had followed the ministry of Jesus for about two years. She had been at the crucifixion and had seen where they buried Jesus. Now she was at the tomb early on Sunday morning because those who are "forgiven much, love much." The other women remained there while Mary ran to tell the disciples. In her absence an angel told the women that Jesus had risen.

John tells us that he and Peter ran to the tomb and he hesitated outside, but Peter went inside to make certain that the body was gone. John then joined him. John believed Jesus was raised, but Peter had to ponder what resurrection meant. These two then went back to Jerusalem, but Mary lingered at the tomb and Mark records that Mary was the first to whom Jesus spoke.

When Mary brought the startling news that the tomb was empty, Peter and John immediately ran from the city to investigate. John ran faster because he was younger, and arriving he did not go into the tomb; however, when Peter reached it, he did not hesitate to enter the burial chamber. He saw the linen clothes in which Jesus had been wrapped still holding its form, but without the body. The face covering was neatly rolled up, indicating the Jesus had taken time to do so. Why? John then entered and noticed that the face napkin was folded and laid in a place by itself, suggesting the casual manner of a person changing clothes. This convinced them that the body had not been removed by the authorities to be buried elsewhere. Peter and John were certain that a resurrection had taken place because of the *hard evidence* before them. They both went back to the Upper Room where they could discuss this new thing.

Luke states that Jesus appeared to two men on the road to Emmaus the afternoon of his resurrection. John also tells us that when these two returned to the Upper Room that same evening to report it to the disciples, Jesus then appeared among them without entering through a door.

Apparent contradictions in the order of these appearances avail nothing to refute the fact that Jesus Christ rose bodily from the grave. Those who had known him before his death were convinced of it.

We are focusing on the life of Simon Peter. This account reveals *why* he came to believe that Jesus had risen from the dead. He had already confessed that he believed Jesus to be the Messiah, but he thought that this meant he would reestablish the Kingdom of David and drive out the Romans. The crucifixion and burial had dashed that hope. Now he had to wrestle with a new concept of the Messiah--a risen Lord.

This simple narrative of John is the style of an *eyewitness*. There is an assuring matter-of-factness about it. John does not say that he saw the Lord in a vision. He tells us of two men running to the tomb and finding undisturbed grave clothes; while standing in an empty tomb. Peter and John were convinced of the *bodily resurrection* because of the very same kind of observation that we rely on in our daily life: they saw it with their own eyes. Notice, however, Jesus did not appear to Peter and John as he did to Mary Magdalene at the tomb.

Application

* We come to believe that Jesus is our Savior for different reasons and circumstances, but we *all must* believe that he was *raised bodily* from the grave. The apostle Paul states that this is the *essence* of the Gospel that produces salvation (I Cor. 15:3; Rom.10:8-10). It is a mockery of God for anyone to state that the resurrection is an allegory of new beginnings.

I grew up in a Baptist church and like so many; I was baptized at age 9 during a revival. But it was only my first step toward Christ. At age 16 I was invited by a childhood friend, Nicky Chavers, to attend a tent revival and sing in the choir. (Years later he became the founder of the Academy of Arts and Logos Theatre in Greenville, SC). The evangelist was a colorful character and very persuasive. After several nights I came under conviction by the Holy Spirit and I knelt with my friend and asked Christ into my life. The following Sunday I was baptized. It was an emotional conversion. I became an avid student of the Scriptures, even taking my Bible to school and studying it rather than my subjects. I went to a denominational college to prepare for ministry and majored in Biblical studies, but all was not well because I was becoming disillusioned with practices I saw in Baptists churches. I became pastor of a small country church and the people were good to my wife and me, but I began to question the reliability of Scripture and the genuineness of my conversion. I lacked assurance of salvation because it was an emotional blur. After talking with my major professor, he encouraged me to go on to seminary because he was confident that it would resolve my doubts. After several years studying the original languages (Hebrew and Greek) and having courses in proofs for the Faith (apologetics), I realized that my faith was not based on *feelings* but on the *fact* of the resurrection of Jesus Christ. I could not be certain about the dating of creation, when dinosaurs lived, Neanderthal man, the extent of Noah's flood, the stories in the OT, but belief in these is *not required* for salvation. Only belief that Jesus is God and that he demonstrated it by rising from the dead (Rom.1:4b) is *necessary* for salvation, and I knew that happened because of its historical documentation in the Four Gospels. All of the rest of the Bible has to center around the resurrection event because that is the *only sign* that Jesus gave to prove his claim of being God (Mt.12:38-41).

* The alleged burial shroud of Jesus kept at the Cathedral in Turin, Italy, is a mystery. An image of a crucified man appears on the cloth, but no one knows how it was made. Scientific tests have been done, but they are inconclusive. Jewish burial customs in the first century meant the body was wrapped with strips of linen cloth from the feet to the neck, like a mummy (Jn.11:44). It was covered with spices to mask the

death odor, but since it was about sundown and the Passover, Nicodemus and Joseph of Arimathea hurriedly placed the body of Jesus in the tomb without completing this procedure (Lk.24:1). A piece of linen cloth was wrapped around Jesus' head to hold the lower jaw in place. Peter and John noticed that the cloth was folded separate from the cloth that encased Jesus' body, which caused them to realize that the body had not been disturbed by Roman soldiers. This causes me to doubt that the Shroud of Turin is authentic because it has a clear facial impression on it, indicating that it covered the head, whereas the biblical text has a face cloth only. Those who believe it is the burial shroud of Jesus do so because they *need* relics in order to believe (e.g. the spear that pierced his side). One of my seminary professors quipped one day, "There are enough splinters of the cross to build a house." That is a good summary of the claim of having relics of Christ and the apostles.

    * I think it is far better to believe in Christ as Savior because the Four Gospels provide a *reliable record* of his life and teachings. John the apostle concluded his Gospel with this statement: "...these are written that you may believe that Jesus is the Christ, the Son of God, and that believing you may have life in his name" Jn.20:31. Those who come to belief simply by reading or studying the Scriptures seem to have a more reasonable, stable faith. They do not fluctuate depending on life circumstances.

    There are only four categories of people with regard to salvation:
1. The unsaved who have no assurance;
2. The saved who have assurance;
3. The saved who lack assurance for several reasons;
4. The unsaved who have a false assurance.

    Only by pondering the resurrection of Jesus as did Simon Peter can a person come to belief in him as Savior and *know* that he is eternally saved.

The apostle John said, "I write these things to you who believe in the name of the Son of God so that you may *know* that you have eternal life...We know also that the Son of God has come and has given us understanding, so that we may know him who is true. And we are *in* him who is true—even in his Son Jesus Christ. He is the true God and eternal life" I Jn.5:13, 20. How much clearer can it be that we can know that we are saved? After all, if a person can be saved and not know it, he can lose it and never miss it.

19 PETER RESTORED
Read: John 21:1-19

Narrative

At the Last Supper Jesus told Peter that he would fall and then be restored (Lk. 22:31,32). After denying three times that he knew Christ, and witnessing the resurrected Christ, it was time now for his *restoration*.

The second week after the resurrection seven of the disciples returned to Galilee because Jesus told Mary to tell them to meet him there (Mk.16:7). While they were waiting Peter decided to return to his trade as a fisherman. Apparently, they could no longer stand to see the fishing boats go out and not take part. These men were not interested in the comforts of city life, the current philosophies, the politics of Rome, or the religious controversies of Judaism. They were comfortable on the lake near their boat, and content to return to their old occupation. These seven men represented the nucleus of believers and if they returned to this obscure village and their fishing business, the world would not hear of the work of Christ they witnessed firsthand. They had no impulse to publish what they knew, and even if they had, they needed to provide for their families, and did not know how they could do it any other way than fishing.

All night they toiled at pulling the net and caught nothing. Just before dawn they were near an unpopulated part of the shore, when they heard a stranger call out, asking if they had caught anything. They were still far enough off shore to cast their net again, so the stranger told them to cast on the other side of the boat. Little did they know that this One had been watching their efforts. The net was so filled that they could not pull it into the boat. Sixty years later John still remembered the number of fishes caught. The point of this miracle, the only one after his resurrection, was to show these men that without him they could not make a living. They might fish all night but would catch nothing. They had committed two or three years earlier to leave fishing and depend on the Lord to provide. By this abundant catch of fishes he showed them that he would provide a living if they would return to fishing for men, as in their *original call* (Lk.5:1-11).

John was the first to recognize Jesus, but it was Peter who jumped into the water to make it to the shore. In every act character shows itself. His impetuousness revealed that his love for Christ was more important than the great catch of fish. When the disciples came ashore they saw that Jesus had already prepared bread and fish on a charcoal fire. They were still not sure that it was Christ because his resurrection body was different. He was already going through a process of glorification that will only be complete after his ascension. This is why there was something strange and mysterious about his appearance. Peter alluded to his experience of eating with the risen Christ in his sermon at the house of Cornelius (Acts 10:41).

After they had eaten, Jesus asked Peter the most

important question one can face. "Simon, do you truly love me more than *these*?" In other words, "Am I to interpret your wading ashore to greet me as an expression that you love me more than you do this fishing business?" Peter replied, "Yes, Lord, you know that I love you." Jesus saw that Peter's previous denial was unpremeditated, a sin of surprise, so he can be forgiven.

Peter had denied knowing the Lord three times, so Jesus asked a second time: "Simon, do you truly love *me*?" This time there was no comparison of the fishing business with his commitment to follow Christ; it was simply about his love for Christ. In this restoration of Peter, the Lord is not testing his conduct, but the heart. Jesus wanted to see if Peter has given an answer out of politeness or sentiment, for if so, it was not genuine.

Jesus was determined to clear away all misunderstanding about Peter's professed love by asking a third time: "Simon, do *you* love me?" He is inviting Peter to search deeply in his heart to ascertain the raw truth. This is the most momentous of all questions one can face from Christ, and Peter answered convincingly.

Three times the Lord told Peter what his *task* should be in the years ahead: "Feed by sheep." This means to give them the word of God so that they can grow to spiritual maturity. This also includes protecting them from heretical teachers (Tend my lambs). Peter never forgot this conversation because at the end of his life he used the same expression as Jesus, "tend my sheep," when he counseled the elders of his churches in Asia Minor about their *responsibility* as pastors (I Pet.5:2). (Notice that he did not tell to *act as priests* on behalf of their people.)

Application

 * The *significance* of this series of questions is this: Christ is about to ascend to the Father and give his work into the hands of these men, leaving the future of his sheep in the keeping of Peter and the rest of the disciples. The one thing he demanded of them was a confession of their love for him because this alone can override selfish ambitions. This love of Christ is what enabled the Apostles to live sacrificially and spread the Gospel throughout the Roman Empire and even as far as India.

 * Did the disciples return to their former life because the past three years seemed surrealistic? Did it all feel like waking from a dream and not knowing if it was real? After all, no one had ever seen the things that they had seen. There are no human categories to compare what they had witnessed with anything else in life. How does one process seeing your dead teacher come back to life and barely recognize him. A person might think that if s/he had seen the miracles Jesus performed that they would never doubt the reality of God. But the memory of witnessing miracles tends to fade. For example, the Jews during the Exodus saw the miracles of God, yet were not confirmed by them. They quickly rebelled against Moses and the Lord on numerous occasions after witnessing these wonderful acts. Maybe the same psychological process was happening with the disciples. I believe they had to return to a "normal life" to sort out their supernatural experiences with Jesus.

 * Over the years I have met too many men who began in ministry but later turned to other things. Some changed their mind in college, others in seminary, or after they began pastoring. Various reasons are given as to why they did not continue: personal problems, conflicts in churches, disappointment with church members, denominational strife, immoral conduct, or lack of financial support. Thousands leave ministry

every year and enter other professions, which means that some denominations are experiencing a shortage of pastors. One of the primary concerns for a person in ministry is whether or not he will be able to provide for his family. Eighty percent of churches have a membership less than 100, which means that most of them do not pay a pastor a living wage. It is not because the members are too poor; rather it is because most of them do not give at least ten percent of their income. This forces a pastor to take a secular job along with pastoring. The members will suffer and not even realize it unless they have experienced the difference it makes when a pastor has time to study and have a word from God for them on Sunday. Often the pastor's wife has to work so that they can live on the *same economic level* as their church members.

* There is too much emphasis today on pastors being formally educated before they go out to serve a church. This can be helpful, but often it has proven to be detrimental. Some have become so educated that they believe nothing in the Bible is to be taken *literally*. It took me ten years to get over my seminary education. Notice, Jesus did not ask if the disciples had great mental ability, or about their knowledge of theology, or how they felt about the duties of ministry. He did not draw up a Creed or a series of articles that they had to sign, nor the type of church government they held to. The primary motivation for serving Jesus is a *sincere* love for him, and the primary *responsibility* is declaring his word to his people ("Feed my Sheep"). Sheep are those who follow the shepherd into "green pastures and by still waters," while goats are independent and go their own way. The pastor is *responsible* for the spiritual well-being of *only* those who sit under his preaching/teaching Sunday-after-Sunday.

* Someone said, "If we are not willing to humble ourselves, the Lord will put us in humbling circumstances until we learn the lesson." The bold

apostle learned *humility* because of his denial of the Lord and having to face him after the resurrection. For this reason, he instructed young pastors, "...be submissive to those who are older [elders]...clothe yourselves with humility, toward one another, because 'God opposes the proud but gives grace to the humble.' Humble yourselves, therefore, under God's mighty hand, that he may lift you up in due time" I Pet.5:5-7. A man is truly great only after his pride is broken. It does not take a psychologist to detect the pompous pride of a pastor.

20   A BOLD PREACHER
Read: Acts 2:14-40

Peter and the six disciples who went with him to Galilee and encountered the risen Lord, returned to Jerusalem to observe the Feast of Pentecost.

At Passover Jews celebrated the Feast of the first ripe grain, the barley harvest. The Priest waved a sheaf before the Lord, sanctifying the harvest and allowing the people to eat of it. Fifty days later it was not a sheaf but a loaf that was offered to signify the completion of the work begun at Passover. Pentecost became the feast of the ingathering of the nations when the Church was born as the Lord's instrument to reap a spiritual harvest. The fact that the Third Person of the Godhead began his earthly ministry on Pentecost signifies that Christianity is connected to and the *completion* of Judaism.

The coming of the Holy Spirit was accompanied

by *external phenomena.* **First**, the "blowing of a mighty rushing wind from heaven." Jesus had compared the moving of the Spirit in regeneration to the wind that blows where it will and only the sound is heard (Jn.3:8). The wind was not outside, it was only in the room. **Second**, tongues of fire rested over the heads of each one in the room and they saw it. John the Baptizer had foretold that the Messiah would "baptize with the Holy Spirit and with fire" (Mt.3:11), and so it was manifest. **Third**, something supernatural was happening because each person was "filled with the Holy Spirit and began to speak in tongues."

A crowd gathered on the street outside the house as these Spirit filled believers poured out of the Upper Room. The multitude was aroused to wonder and wanted to know what these manifestations meant. It was then that Peter stepped forward to exercise the "keys to the kingdom." Baptism is pressed upon the multitude as a *present duty*, and as a result there were three thousand baptized that day. Peter opened the door of the kingdom to the Jews on the day of Pentecost, and later the door to the Gentiles by the conversion and baptism of Cornelius.

There are several things about the sermon we should note. **One,** the *outspoken tone* is evidence of the power and influence of the Holy Spirit on Peter. Here he was standing up and proclaiming a risen and glorfied Jesus just seven weeks after he was crucified. This man who had turned coward before a maid's accusation, now declared boldly that Jesus of Nazareth, whom they condemned, was God's Son. This *psychological change* in Peter, and the other believers, is one of the strongest proofs of the resurrection of Christ and the coming of the Holy Spirit.

Two, the sermon also indicates that Peter had a *new spiritual insight.* The explanation of prophecies by the resurrected Christ (Lk.24:44-48) enabled Peter to see OT prophecies through new eyes. There is no indication from the Gospels that Peter knew these OT prophecies to be Messianic. Peter also related the coming of the Holy Spirit to a prophecy of Joel, which he had not understood before.

Three, he appealed to the *facts* about the death of Christ. The people saw or heard what happened at his trial and crucifixion, so it was not necessary for Peter to describe it. He simply charged them with being guilty of killing the Son of God.

Four, he applied the words of David (Ps.16:8-11) to Jesus. This *method of interpreting the OT* would be used by the apostles to prove that Jesus was the Messiah throughout their mission journeys (Acts 17:1-4). Indeed, Jesus himself set the precedent for this use of the OT when he explained to the two disciples on the road to Emmaus "what was said in all the Scriptures (OT) about himself" (Lk.24:27).

Finally, when the multitude was under conviction by the Holy Spirit and cried out asking what they should do, Peter told them, "*Repent and be baptized*, everyone of you in the name of Jesus Christ for the forgiveness of your sins. And you will receive the gift of the Holy Spirit." Both John the Baptizer and Jesus had preached repentance and baptism, and now Peter calls for the same. Repentance meant a change of direction in one's life, and water baptism illustrated the cleansing from sin. Baptism was the door into the Church. The position that baptism occupies in apostolic teaching is worthy of careful study.

Application
*   Not only is the Christian movement attested by NT documents, a Roman historian from the same time as the apostles, Tacitus wrote, "Christus, from whom the name Christian has its origin, suffered the extreme penalty [i.e. crucifixion] during the reign of Tiberius at the hands of one of our procurators, Pontius Pilate, and a most mischievous superstition [i.e. Christianity], thus

checked for the moment, *again broke out* in Judea
Annals, book xv. chap.44. So, this Roman historian,
who knew nothing of Christ except what he read in the
imperial archives at Rome, agreed with the Gospels and
Acts that the Christian movement appeared to be ended
by the death of Christ, but came back strong when the
apostles' preached that Jesus arose from the dead.

  * Pentecost was a onetime event. Just as the
Second Person of the Godhead, who was a Spirit Being,
added humanity to deity in becoming Jesus Christ, even
so, the Third Person of the Godhead, who was Spirit,
added humanity by indwelling every believer. At
Christmas we celebrate the incarnation of the Son; at
Pentecost we celebrate the *incarnation* of the Holy
Spirit. He created a new body of Christ—the Church.
Those who hope God will send new Pentecostal
manifestations are expecting something that will not
happen. The Spirit does move in power among
believers in certain times and places, but the
phenomena of Pentecost has not happened since the
death of the apostles. What is passed off as Pentecostal
experiences is nothing more than an emotionally
induced dissociative disorder or outright fakery.

  * Much controversy has arisen over "speaking in
tongues." This passage is the source of a serious error--
speaking in tongues as a *sign of sanctification*. While
pastoring in Southeast Missouri during the 70s the
charismatic movement swept through the area. As a
result, Bible study groups sprang up in surrounding
communities. I was invited to teach three of these
groups on weeknights. People who sat in pews for
years and had no interest in going deeper into God's
word were now willing to sit for two hours with an
open Bible and take notes. They believed that "speaking
in tongues" was a sign of the "baptism in the Spirit."
Some of them urged me to seek the experience by
lingering in prayer and relaxing with my head tilted

back and opening my mouth so that I could learn to speak the heavenly language. My response was: I want all the Lord has for me, but this does not seem to fit with what happened at Pentecost. They were advocating an ecstatic utterance that every believer should seek. My reasoning was: If it is a gift of God why was it necessary to seek it? It was exactly the same error believers at Corinth held and that Paul had corrected. Over the three-year period that I taught them they began to gradually understand the gifts and their purpose. They backed away from emphasizing the tongues experience and focused on growing up spiritually by feeding on God's word and exercising *all* the gifts of ministry.

I take "speaking in tongues" as an *ability to speak the gospel in* a *known language* that one has never studied. The apostle Paul interpreted the prophecy of Isaiah (28:11,12) about the Jews hearing the gospel in other languages as being fulfilled in speaking in tongues (I Cor.14:21). In God's *providence* the Jewish people had been scattered over the Mediterranean world, so that when these Jews returned home after Pentecost they carried the gospel with them. The human tongue, sanctified by fire from the Holy Spirit, became the instrument for the spread of the gospel.

* Notice: Peter did not lead the crowd in a prayer asking Jesus to come into their hearts. This is a common practice among evangelicals. Many church members date their salvation experience from the time of the "sinner's prayer" rather than their baptism. Nowhere in the NT is anyone told to pray to receive Christ as Savior. The emphasis is on "repenting and believing the gospel" (Mark 1:15). When Peter told the crowd to "Repent and be baptized" he is not teaching that water baptism saves, rather, he is saying that it is the *unique means* of publicly confessing Christ as Savior. The act of baptism nails down the time and place that the believer committed their life to Christ as Savior. When Martin

Luther was assaulted by the Devil, all he could say was, "I was baptized." In other words, salvation is not a private matter of asking Jesus into one's heart. It is based on belief in Christ and the act of baptism, rather than a subjective feeling. No wonder that so many professed Christians have *no assurance of salvation* when it is based on simply repeating a prayer. True saving faith looks to the work of Christ and the fact of baptism for assurance. This is the basis for perseverance in the face of doubt and difficulties. The believer might backslide, but his journey of faith over a lifetime will not end in unbelief.

　　* Another modern twist is that a person does not need to repent of sins; he only needs to believe the Gospel to become a Christian. This view explains why there are so many professed Christians who live no differently than non-Christians. Their moral views and practices are the same. This concept so dilutes the message of Christianity that people can no longer distinguish between true Christians and those who are just think they are. A person who is truly a Christian will live a *changed* life. S/he cannot continue in a life of sin because it is contrary to the Holy Spirit's work of sanctification. A true believer *must* and *will* repent and turn away from his former sinful practices.

21 AN UNDENIABLE HEALING
Read: Acts 3:1-10

The time that lapsed from Pentecost to the first healing by Peter was probably a few weeks. The Apostles had plenty to do with the thousands that came into the Church on Pentecost. These new Christians needed to learn about Christ and his teachings so that they would be rooted and grounded in the Faith (Heb.2:3). As Jewish converts they already knew the OT, so it was simply a matter of taking that information and showing how Jesus fulfilled it.

The Apostles and the early Church had not yet separated from the Temple and Judaism (Luke 24:53). That would not happen until the Romans destroyed it in 70 A.D. At that point Judaism and Christianity became *antagonistic.* The Jewish system was beginning to be regarded as obsolete and superseded by Christianity even before the Temple was destroyed. (Theme of the Book of Hebrews) There is no indication that these Jewish Christians continued offering sacrifices at the Temple. Such would have denied the sacrifice of Christ.

The scene of this first apostolic miracle is simple enough. Peter and John went to the Temple to pray about 3 p.m. A cripple who lay everyday at the Beautiful gate to beg, asked for a donation. The Temple was not like a Cathedral; one first went through the Court of the Gentiles (i.e. a plaza), then through the Beautiful Gate into the Court of the Women. Peter told the man to walk in the name of Jesus Christ, then helped him stand up. The healed man entered Solomon's Porch "walking and leaping and praising God" with Peter and John. Jesus had taught here (Jn.10:23) and Jewish believers used it as a gathering place (Acts 5:12). A crowd, which knew the man as a beggar because he was a cripple, ran together in excitement to learn what happened. Again, Peter with the "keys of the kingdom" preached his second sermon.

The sermon has four parts. **First**, he pointed out that he was not the healer, that Jesus Christ did it (vss.12,16). Peter took the greatest care to emphasize that he had no power in himself to heal anyone. **Second**, he directed the people's attention to what they had done to Jesus only a few months before (vss.13-15). He used a 2nd person plural "you" to charge the crowd with the collective murder of Jesus. This produced guilt and shame in the hearers. **Third**, he reviewed Jewish history and pointed out that Jesus was its fulfillment (vss.16-25). **Finally**, he called on them to respond to what God had provided for them in Christ (vs.26).

Application

* All the components of a *good sermon* are found in Peter's message. Main line churches are in decline because of a lack of good preaching. Much of what passes as a sermon today is actually nothing more than a lecture, a devotional talk, a testimony, or a pep talk.

A *lecture* from the pulpit is much like one in the University classroom. People listen passively and take notes. The pastor has extensive notes from which he reads, seldom changing inflections in his voice or motioning with his hands. It is usually informative, but very dry. This preaching produces cerebral Christians that do not get emotionally involved with the message.

The *devotional* is not over fifteen minutes and is very soft on theology. It is intended to inspire the hearers to live better and help others. Actually, it is rooted in a humanistic philosophy that makes everyone feel better. The pastor is careful not to say anything that might offend anyone. People who do not want to think about serious issues are drawn to this kind of message. Many main line churches have a steady diet of devotional messages.

A *testimony* is "What the Lord has done for me." It is very personal and often characterized by a mixture of tears and joy. The hearers are drawn into the speaker's religious experiences; usually without any basis in Scripture. These are "touchy/feely" talks designed to encourage others to be open to mystical experiences. This kind of message is often heard during spiritual retreats.

Pep talks, like given by a coach in the locker room, are common among Pentecostals, Charismatics and in Black churches. The preacher usually takes several verses and becomes very emotional about them in order to hype the congregation until they *feel like* they are worshipping. The people often wave their hands in the air, hold their heads back with eyes closed, sway back and forth, moan and cry, which resembles a pagan religious orgy. They leave feeling good, but it does not last. It is similar to drug addiction because they must come back every Sunday to "get high." They need another "fix" in order to make it through the coming week. Confusion and chaos characterize these gatherings. Year-after-year they are conditioned by the *emotional frenzy* to remain immature and unstable Christians. Such *exhibitionism* is contrary to the dictum of Paul that "everything [in worship] should be done in a fitting and proper way" I Cor.14:40.

The most effective sermon is an exposition of Scripture with application to the current circumstances of life so that people can develop God's perspective of reality and act accordingly. It has a real bite to it, even to the degree of the congregation being uncomfortable with what they are hearing because it produces conviction. Preaching is the word of God coming through *human personality*. Worshippers sit quietly and listen with an open Bible to confirm that what the pastor is preaching is true. Such a practice of preaching and listening produces spiritually mature believers that do not fluctuate up and down in the Christian life.

* Christianity is firmly rooted in *time* and *place*. Peter made a declaration of certain *historical facts*. University professors, the media, and liberal pastors might speak of Christianity's spiritual ideals or its moral

principles, but doubt its historical veracity. Some
regard the stories as poetry or legend. The New
Testament documents, upon which Christianity is
based, are more reliable than any other ancient
documents (e.g. Homer's Illiad), therefore, they should
be taken seriously. Some dismiss the Four Gospels
because they are "religious documents." But how would
anyone write about the life and works of Jesus without
persuading others to believe he is God? The Four
Gospels stand in starke contrast to the Gnostic gospels
(about 50), because they are only *fictional* accounts
(written 150 or 200 years after the life of Christ) that
were produced to co-opt Christianity. If the *eyewitness*
accounts as set forth in the Four Gospels (most written
before 60 A.D.) are rejected, we end up with a
Christianity in name and appearance only. Such a
liberal Christianity might sustain the soul when all is
well, but when one's life is falling apart, or the nation
lies in ruins, or one faces sickness and death, one needs
the solid realities of fact and truth.

   * Once again Pentecostalism errs, as it does on
"speaking in tongues," by teaching that healings are as
available today as they were in the days of the apostles.
They often quote the passage in Hebrews 13:8: "Jesus
Christ is the same yesterday, today and forever," to
support their view. This verse is speaking about the
nature of Christ as unchanging, not about how he
chooses to work in the world. It is clear from biblical
history that God uses *different methods* to reveal himself
at different places and times. Miracles are *not* his
primary method; in fact, they are rare in Scripture. Only
Moses, Elijah, and Elisha performed miracles, then Jesus
and only three apostles did miracles, which proves how
brief was the time period. After the death of the
apostles, miracles did not happen in the early church.
Yet, Pentecostals claim that miracles happen today if a
person has enough faith. And of course, if a miracle
does not happen it is because the person failed to
believe, which produces great guilt. In context, the

verse in Hebrews is contrasting the changing lives of their pastors with the unchangeable nature of Christ. There are reports of healings *on the order of* those in Acts in areas of the world where the Gospel is newly being proclaimed. It seems that the Lord allows such healings in order to *gain* a *hearing for the Gospel*, much as in the ministry of Jesus and the Apostles. But after the Gospel has been established and local churches formed, miraculous healings cease.

(I actually sympathize with Pentecostals in that I wish "signs, wonders, and powers" were possible today because I could fill the largest sanctuary if several miracles happened during a worship service where I was ministering.)

22   PETER'S SERMON AND ARREST
Read: Acts 4:1-22

Peter and John had their first encounter with the Jewish authorities because of the cripple man being healed. This miracle was not only an act of compassion on the man, it was the *means* by which the Gospel could be presented to the Sanhedrin, the highest authority in Judaism.

While Peter was preaching, the priests and the captain of the Temple guards (Malchus, whose ear he had cut off?) and some Sadducees mingled in the crowd. They heard him proclaiming the resurrection of Jesus Christ. The Sadducees did not believe the Five Books of Moses taught life after death. They were special antagonists of Jesus throughout his ministry because he taught that the faithful live with God forever in new bodies. Because Peter and John testified of the risen and glorified Lord, they were in direct opposition to the central doctrine of Sadducees that denied the future life. It is no wonder the new teaching concerning a risen Messiah excited them; it undercut their basic doctrine. No Sadducee is mentioned in the NT as converting to Christianity, whereas some of the Pharisees did because they believed the same as Peter about the resurrection. If what Peter was preaching was true, then the Sadducees were wrong and they knew it. The resurrection of Jesus was obvious and this is what the apostles preached.

Peter and John were arrested by the Temple guards and locked in a room in the Temple area. The next morning, they were brought before the Sanhedrin which met daily after the morning sacrifice. The Sanhedrin consisted of seventy-one members, comprising chief priests, elders of the people, and most renowned rabbis. They sat in a semicircle, with the president in the center, while opposite were three benches for the scholars of Jewish Law. The court was composed largely of Sadducees, with a few Pharisees. It was before this group of inquisitors that Peter and John were brought to explain the healing.

Peter needed the filling of the Holy Spirit to speak with *conviction*, and it happened again as at Pentecost. He spoke so boldly and clearly that the Sanhedrin could not refute what he said. Jesus had warned the disciples that such would happen: "But when they arrest you, do not worry about what to say or how to say it. At that time you will be given what to say, for it will not be you speaking, but the Spirit of your Father speaking through you" Mt.10:19,20. The court dismissed the prisoners while it decided what to do. Keep in mind that these are the same men who condemned Jesus just a few months earlier. Since it was so obvious that the crippled man was healed, they could not deny it; all that was left was to forbid them to speak in the name of Jesus.

Peter and John returned to the company of believers and reported what the Lord had done. They offered prayer and praise to God for giving them the opportunity to speak the Gospel boldly to a court that could have put them to death. They also asked, "Now Lord, consider the threats and enable your servants to speak your word with great boldness. Stretch out your hand to heal and perform miraculous signs and wonders through the name of your holy servant Jesus" vss.29,30. The place they were praying was shaken (a mini earthquake?) as an indication from the Lord that he had heard their prayer.

Application

* It is clear from Peter's defense that apostolic Christianity is a *system of belief* based on the bodily resurrection of Jesus. It is neither a philosophical system of thought, nor a system of ethical teaching, and it is not a symbolical idea typifying a soul being renewed as liberals contend, if so, the Sadducees would not have troubled themselves to oppose such teachings. Liberal Christianity today has emasculated the apostolic message and made it devoid of any real foundation in historical fact. It has become a social message about doing good in the community and the world. If Christianity as proclaimed by Peter was of the modern type, why was it bitterly opposed by the Sadducees? They understood that Peter preached a Jesus Christ literally raised from the dead and ascended into a life that they denied.

* Jesus promised the disciples that the Holy Spirit would *speak for them* when on trial. Some have taken this to mean that a preacher should not prepare a sermon ahead of time. It is amazing that these supposedly spontaneous sermons consist of clichés that are repeated in each sermon. This is not a promise authorizing preachers to dispense with careful thought

and deep study. When applying the great truths of Scripture to the circumstances of modern life, a preacher must use discernment. In the case of Peter, it is a case of immediate and direct inspiration. However, preachers today, with all the resources available, must use study, organization, meditation, life experiences, as means through which inspiration comes. It is a lack of respect for the hearers when a preacher speaks without adequate preparation to hold their attention. My sermon preparation includes all these elements, in addition to writing out the sermon to have good word use and avoid repetition. Winston Churchill spent thirty hours of writing in order to speak thirty minutes. Should a preacher do any less? My written sermons have become a collection of books that are now available at Amazon in print and Kindle as ebooks.

   * One might ask, "How could the Sadducees witness the miracle of healing and not conclude that God had done a work of power?" The Sanhedrin did not deny that a miracle had been performed, but it did not lead them to belief in Jesus Christ. They simply inquired as to the *power of the name* by which the miracle had occurred. These Jewish leaders were familiar with magicians and exorcists doing unexplainable things. They believed that supernatural things happened, but the question was, "What was the source of power?" These same men did not deny the miracles of Jesus, they simply dismissed them as being caused by demons (Mt.12:24). Did Peter do the miracle by demonic power, or a secret name of God? Neither, said Peter, "It was by the name of Jesus Christ of Nazareth, whom you crucified but whom God raised from the dead" vs.10. The Sanhedrin understood the implications of this and forbade them to preach and heal in the name of Jesus (4:17; 5:28,40). Peter was very bold in setting forth the power of Jesus' name because of the Holy Spirit speaking through him.

   * Peter expressed the apostolic position that

salvation is in none other than Jesus Christ (vs.12). As the apostles went out preaching the Gospel and encountered other religions, they did not regard them as other ways of knowing God; indeed, they declared that demons were the power behind other religions. The *test* for Christian orthodoxy is the apostolic view, that Jesus is the *only way* to know the One True God (Jn.17:3). They, no doubt, based their belief on Jesus' statement: "I am the way and the truth and the life. No one comes to the Father except through me" Jn.14:6. It is understandable that non-Christians would not believe that Jesus is the only way of salvation, but why do people who profess to be Christians believe that salvation can be found in other religions. Such people do not want to offend those who practice other religions, so they compromise and allow other ways of salvation. But if salvation was available in other religions, then God did an *unnecessary* thing by sending his only Son to die. Jesus even pleaded with his Father to find another way of salvation other than his death on the cross (Mt.26:39,42), but it was not to be because he alone was righteous enough to die for the sins of humanity (I Jn.2:2) and secure salvation for those who repent and believe in him. Paul said that if a person can be saved by keeping the law of Moses, then Christ died in vain (Gal.2:21), and that applies to all other religions. Liberals also think it necessary to *accommodate the message to the culture* to make it acceptable. It is now obvious that when an *exclusive* Gospel is presented, the name of Jesus is still as much an offense to the world as it was to the Sanhedrin. This is why Christians have been persecuted throughout history and continue to be in almost every nation.

23 APOSTOLIC DISCIPLINE
Read: Acts 4:32-5:11

Several years passed and the church at Jerusalem

grew to over five thousand. The population of the city was probably around a hundred thousand. Believers continued to meet on Solomon's Porch at the Temple, as well as in homes throughout the city.

By this time the Jewish population was opposing the Christian movement, even though it was regarded by Rome as a *sect* of Judaism. Non-believing Jews began to avoid buying or selling to fellow Jewish Christians. This caused them to lose their businesses, but it also drove them together. The writer of Hebrews, addressing these Jewish Christians, alluded to this persecution (Heb. 10:32-34). James, as the pastor of the Jerusalem church, speaks about poverty and helping fellow church members (James 2:14-17). John was also in the Jerusalem church and addressed the issue of social concern for needy believers (I Jn.3:17). Hence, the sharing of possessions was an integral part of the early Christian community (Acts 4:32-37). Each family still had ownership of their property and goods but they were open handed in sharing with believers as they saw a need. Caring for brothers and sisters in Christ was an expression of the *unity* the Spirit had created among them. Because of the economic sanctions by the hostile Jews the poverty became so great that later on the apostle Paul took a collection from the Gentile churches in order to help the Jerusalem church (Rom.15:25-27; I Cor.16:1-4).

The apostles remained in Jerusalem in order to minister among the thousands of new converts. Peter is one of the leaders of the church, along with James, the half-brother of Jesus (Gal.1:18-20). A *central authority* was forming around the apostles.

One of the men in the church, Barnabas, owned some property and sold it in order to give to the needy in the church. He was a key figure in the growth of the Jerusalem church. Later on he introduced Paul to the apostles there and became a fellow missionary with him.

A couple, Ananias and Sapphira, followed Barnabas' example, but their actions do not arise from pure motives. Maybe they desired recognition from the congregation. They sold some property but did not give the whole amount as promised. Rather, they kept back some of it for themselves. When Ananias brought the money so that the apostles could distribute it, Peter had spiritual discernment enough to know that he was being deceptive. He sensed the gravity of the situation because Satan was the source of this lie, and that it was not just against the church, but against God. Ananias fell dead. Notice, it was God, not Peter who sentenced Ananias to death. He was taken out and buried. Then three hours later Sapphira came in, not knowing her husband died, and repeated the lie. Peter pronounced judgment on her and she also died immediately and was buried (Acts 5:1-10).

The result of this is that fear, not in the sense of terror, but of *reverential awe* for God the Spirit and his power as displayed through the apostle Peter.

Application

* Here is an example of how a chapter division hinders the correct interpretation of a passage. A chapter should consist of a unit of thought, but in the present form it does not do so. If a person begins reading at chapter five he thinks the problem of Ananias and Sapphire was only about them deceiving the church and lying to God. However, if a person begins reading at 4:32 s/he understands the background of their sin. They were guilty of *breaking the unity* of the church by their deception, and for that God judged them. The

chapter should end at 5:11 and a new chapter (6) begin because it takes up a new unit of thought.

     * To break the spiritual unity of a church is a serious matter. What damage would have been done to the early church if Peter had not stopped this hypocrisy? It might have caused a split in the Jerusalem church. The apostle Paul warned believers at Corinth: "Don't you know that you yourselves are God's temple and that God's Spirit lives in you? If anyone destroys God's temple, God will destroy him; for God's temple is sacred, and you are that temple" I Cor.3:16,17. The temple here is not the physical body (I Cor. 6:19), rather it is the body of believers. God lives among believers as he did in Solomon's temple, and to desecrate the spiritual body (local church) is to risk God's discipline.

     Many churches of main line denominations are now dividing over the issues of same sex marriage and ordination of practicing homosexuals. Much hurt is experienced in these church divisions. Some want to avoid the issue, hoping it will go away with time. But Christians should not settle for a false peace at any price. When a church or denomination has obviously turned away from the teachings of the apostles, which those who approve of homosexuality are doing, it is *right* to separate and form a new church or join a denomination that refuses to compromise Scripture to accommodate cultural changes.

     * Peter exercised *apostolic authority* in calling this couple to account for their sinful act. If he had not handled the problem, would this couple have continued to pretend to be living righteous lives? The apostle Paul instructed the church at Corinth to dismiss a man for having sexual relations with his stepmother (I Cor.5). They were reluctant to do so for fear of not being tolerant. Churches today do not discipline members for even the grossest of sins. It would also be tough love to dismiss members who practice immorality or are inactive in the church.

* The *contest* is not between Peter and Anania; it is between Satan and the Holy Spirit. The Spirit had created unity in the fellowship and Satan used this couple to destroy it. Later in life Peter warned believers that the "devil prowls around like a roaring lion looking for someone to devour" (I Pet.5:8). Whether Ananias and Sapphira were false believers or true, they were taken advantage of by Satan in order to destroy the unity created by the Holy Spirit, and for this they were severely judged. Notice that Peter equated lying to the Spirit as being the same as lying to God (cf.4b and 9a).

* Because some Christians have a misconception about the nature of God, they do not think God will put them to death for *deliberate* sin. If a person's concept of God is not the biblical concept of God, the person is worshipping a false god. The Bible clearly teaches that God is love, but He is also *holy* and has anger against sin. He judged Ananias and his wife because of their hypocrisy. They played the hypocrite at the very time when the Spirit had poured out his grace and power upon the Jerusalem church. The formation of the church during the life of the apostles was an *exceptional time*. We do not live in a time when the Spirit is moving in such power, therefore, church members are able to be hypocritical and get by with it. If God were to take out every hypocrite at church next Sunday, the following week would be taken up with funerals.

24 KINGDOMS IN CONFLICT
Read: Acts 4:23-37; 5:12-42

The Christian community praised God for the

release of Peter and John from arrest. Even though the Sanhedrin warned them not to preach or heal in the name of Jesus, this did not stop them. Believers asked the Lord to continue to perform signs and wonders because it gave them an opportunity to preach to the crowds (4:30). Apparently, the Lord answered because the apostles performed miracles, signs and wonders among the people. The apostle Peter was so full of the Holy Spirit that miracles similar to those Jesus performed happened through him. As a result, many people in Jerusalem became believers. The Jewish authorities could no longer ignore what was happening in their midst because the movement had grown so large.

The Sanhedrin took action by having the apostles arrested again, but during the night an angel of the Lord opened the jail doors and instructed them to go preach the gospel in the Temple. When the Sanhedrin gathered the next morning to hear their cases, it was reported that the apostles were not in jail; in fact, they were preaching in the Temple courtyard. The captain of the Temple guards arrested them and brought them immediately before the Sanhedrin.

Peter, as leader of the apostles, used the "keys" again to make their defense. He stated a very basic principle: There is a *higher law* than any human court. As before, he accused the Sanhedrin of being responsible for the death of Jesus. This, of course, infuriated the court and prompted them to call for the death of the apostles. Gamaliel, a highly respected Pharisee, cooled their tempers by reminding them that letting the matter run its course was wiser, because in the past false Messiahs came to nothing. The Sanhedrin was persuaded, so the apostles were flogged with 39 ashes and released with orders not to preach in the name of Jesus.

The apostles responded to their ordeal by rejoicing that they could suffer for Christ. They even continued to preach in the Temple and from house to house that Jesus was the Jewish Messiah.

Application:
     * We must consider the attitude of the apostles toward religious and state authorities to know how to respond to our government. Peter himself said toward the end of his life: "Submit yourselves for the Lord's sake to every authority instituted among men: whether to the king as the supreme authority, or to governors, who are sent by him to punish those who do wrong and to commend those who do right" 1 Pet.2:13,14. Keep in mind that he is saying this while living under one of the most evil of Roman Emperors, Nero. The State was established by God to control the sinfulness of man through laws (I Tim.1:8-11) and police/military power (Rom. 13:4). On the local level, the Sanhedrin had authority from God to keep order in Israel by judging the wicked and honoring the good. But we see that the table has turned, they were punishing the good and letting the wicked off. In *ordinary times* Christians are to be obedient citizens, but what are Christians to do when the State becomes evil? (e.g. Nazi Germany)
     The State can/does/has certainly become evil. As the answer of the apostles indicates, the Lordship of Christ may conflict with the demands of the government. Some Christians think the government deserves *unquestioning obedience.* Revelation 13 and 18 indicate that the State can become an enemy of God and dominated by injustice and materialism. When this begins to happen, Christians must speak out and take action. Other Christians go to the opposite extreme of believing that any form of government is *inevitably an evil institution* that must be distrusted and resisted. A

balanced view is that God ordained government so that humans could live in community in peace, but when it becomes evil it has *lost its divine sanction.*

Peter adds a caveat that is often overlooked: "Live as free men, but do not use your freedom as a cover up for evil; live as servants of God" I Pet.2:16. If the State tries to restrict the freedom of the Christian to live as such and reach others with the gospel, it should be opposed (e.g.England). We are approaching this situation because religious freedom is now being interpreted as applying only *within* the four walls of the church building, not in the work place or the public square. Christians should exhaust every resource available to stand against any government rule that restricts the free exercise of their conscience to worship and witness of Christ. This is what Peter and John did before the Sanhedrin.

Where does the reader's loyalty lie? To the State or the Kingdom of God? The apostle Paul reminded the Christians in Philippi that their "citizenship is in heaven" in contrast to the way unbelievers conduct themselves in the world, Phil.3:18-20. Even though these Christians were subject to the Roman State, it was secondary to their true allegiance to King Jesus. It was said of the apostles that "they are all defying Caesar's decrees, saying that there is another king, one called Jesus" Acts 17:7. Would this society say the same of us?

We must speak up boldly like Peter before the Sanhedrin or we will lose our freedoms. Maybe it is time we elevated the Christian flag above the American flag in our worship places and recite: "I pledge allegiance to the Christian flag, and to the Savior for whose kingdom it stands, one Savior, crucified, risen, and coming again, with life and liberty for all who believe" to show that Jesus is our King rather than the U.S. government.

* Like many religious leaders today, the Sanhedrin was more concerned about keeping their position of power than seeking the Truth regardless of

the cost. Gamaliel's counsel might have spared the lives of the apostles, but it was *not* the noble course he should have taken. His was the kind of advice always given by men who do not want to commit themselves to a position. He should have recommended that the Sanhedrin do an investigation of the truth-claims made by the apostles, but he did not have the moral courage to do the right thing.

Compromise is the recourse of moral cowards. I have a friend who attended a Baptist college in preparation for ministry. He especially liked one of the professors and took as many classes under him as possible. Perry soon found a position on the staff of a local church as youth pastor. Not long afterward the senior pastor resigned and that same professor came as interim. Perry had been doing some cutting-edge ministry with the youth that he had learned in the professor's class and the young people responded in overwhelming numbers. It was not long, however, before some of the deacons called into question his methods. The matter was brought to the professor who was acting as interim pastor. The professor who had told Perry in the classroom to be courageous and bold in ministry betrayed him by calling for him to conform to the desires of the deacons. Perry resigned and left the ministry because he saw that when pressure comes from some of the members, pastors usually fold.

25 A SORCERER EXPOSED
Read: Acts 8:9-25

The Jerusalem Church found in necessary to ordain seven men (Acts 6:5,6) to oversee the distribution of goods to needy widows. One of these, Stephen, became so powerful in performing miracles and preaching, that the Sanhedrin arrested him and, after a hearing, ordered that he be stoned to death. Paul was instrumental is this execution.

Another deacon, Philip, became a missionary to the Samaritans. Persecution of the church in Jerusalem was so strong that many of its members left the city, and in doing so spread the gospel. Phillip reached out beyond Jerusalem to preach the gospel to Samaritans, a mixed race of Jews and Gentiles. The Jews despised them. Their religion, however, was based on the Five Books of Moses, which meant that they had similarities with Jewish worship. This was evident in Jesus' conversation with the woman at Jacob's well (Jn.4:4,20,21). Phillip had power to do signs and perform healings in order to *confirm* his message was from God. As a result, many of the Samaritans believed the gospel and were baptized. One of them was Simon the Great, a sorcerer with a reputation in the area.

Even though these new believers were baptized, they had not received the Holy Spirit. So, the church in Jerusalem sent Peter and John to investigate why the Spirit had not accompanied baptism. The Holy Spirit came when Peter and John laid hands on them. We are not told what the manifestation was that proved the Holy Spirit had come in power (tongues or prophesying?), but whatever it was convinced everyone present that something supernatural had taken place.

Simon, who was accustomed to buying tricks from other magicians, wanted to purchase the ability to give the Holy Spirit to people. Peter gave a strong rebuke that revealed the true condition of Simon's heart as a person who was not regenerated by the Spirit.

Application
* A new function was created in order to take care of the *practical needs* in the church. Deacons were given the task of overseeing the distribution of food to widows. These persons should have the gift of service (I Pet.4:10) but it often becomes the good-old-boy system. Most denominations recognize the function of deacons. These persons are prone to become the power brokers in the church. Baptist churches are known for splitting over trivial matters. This is due partly to their spiritual immaturity, but also due to their failure to follow the biblical pattern of having both elders and deacons. The early church had elders to oversee the *spiritual* life of the church and deacons to see to the *functional* aspects.

* There is a mystery in the text. Would the Lord permit his people to be persecuted in order to get them to fulfill the commission to go out and preach the gospel? It appears that is precisely what the Lord did in the persecution of believers in Jerusalem. Several years had passed since Pentecost and they had not gone out into all the world preaching. They had gotten comfortable and did not want to go into new territory. It seems cruel to us that the Lord worked in such a way because we have the concept that the Lord should protect his people. Maybe it is more important that the gospel go out than his people enjoy comfortable worship.

* The sorcerer Simon must have had *demonic power* working through him in order to influence the city of Samaria that he was great. Even though the word "magic" means an illusionist, that is not what Simon was doing. He was deceiving the people through Satanic power in order to keep them in bondage. Simon had entered into an alliance with evil spirits to bend the people to his will (e.g. The Harry Potter series). This

was more than superstition on the part of the people; it was real. We refer to this as *occult* practices.

The fact that Phillip could do great signs and miracles indicated that there was another source of power. So, it is not just the ability to work miracles, it is the *message* which accompanies it that indicates the source of the power. Phillip preached the "good news of the kingdom of God" and introduced people to it by baptism. Simon was able to do works that convinced the people that he had supernatural power, but his *message was false*. Since the age of reason most people regard Simon's power over the Samaritans to their superstitious nature. Sophisticated people no longer believe in demons doing signs and wonders. All that has been explained away by psychology. Demons are only the stuff of horror movies, they think.

One of the things seminary did not prepare me for, was how to face demonic opposition. Over the years I have encountered people who threatened me for exposing their sins. Some of it was veiled while other statements were direct. If I had not recognized the source as demonic I might have blinked. But I stood firm and countered the threat with biblical authority. The growing hostility to Christianity in the public sector, the proliferation of cults, the increase of gross immorality or the belief in no moral code, are indicators of demonic activity.

Justin Martyr wrote that Simon (c.150) was the first Gnostic heretic. He reported that Simon went to Rome during the time of Claudius Caesar and died there on orders from Nero.

   * Ordination to ministry by the laying on of hands has a history in the OT (Num.11:16; 27:18-23; Deut.34:9). The apostles naturally used this symbol upon the appointment of these first elders (Acts 14:23) and deacons. Paul reminded Timothy certain powers were conveyed to him by the laying on of hands (2 Tim.1:6). It is *symbolic* of the transmission of function

and authority in ministry and should not be done with a spiritually immature believer (I Tim.5:22). Paul said to the elders at Ephesus that they were *given authority* in ministry by the Holy Spirit at ordination (Acts 20:28).

Something happened to me as a result of ordination. I went before my home church in Pensacola at age 16 and told them that I had a desire to preach. While in college a country church called me as pastor. They wrote a letter to my home church requesting my ordination. The date was set for March 8, 1964. The pastor called together an ordination council to examine my doctrines and life before the congregation. After doing so, the council adjourned and made a decision to ordain me. I preached a short sermon and then the council gathered around me as I knelt at the altar. They laid hands on me and prayed over me. I was given a Bible and charged to go forth and preach the word. Eighteen faded signatures are on my ordination certificate. I value their trust in me to pastor God's people. I was invited by a Presbyterian church in 1995 to be interim pastor. The session said that I needed to be ordained by them to be official. I refused because I was not ordained to a denomination; I was ordained to the Gospel ministry, to be exercised wherever there is an open door.

I believe authority to preach was given to me in that service which I would not have had otherwise. Some have sensed that in my preaching. A church member once said to me, "You are a different man when you step into the pulpit." He was referring to the *authority* with which I speak when delivering God's word. I had a sense that the Holy Spirit was speaking through you. I know it when it is happening. As an older black pastor said to the seminary professor who was instructing the students to remain calm and dignified in the pulpit: "Something gets hold of me when I preach and I can't stay calm."

    *   Jesus told the disciples that when the Holy Spirit

98

came in power the gospel would be preached in "Jerusalem, Judea and Samaria, and the utter most parts of the earth." Those are the *three phases* for the spread of the gospel. The Holy Spirit came on the believers in Jerusalem, the **first** phase, now he is descending on believers in Samaria, the **second** phase. The apostles were the *official persons* to introduce the Holy Spirit into each phase. This is the reason there are only three places in Acts where the Holy Spirit comes on believers with external phenomena. The **third** phase is when Paul came to Ephesus and found believers who had not received the Holy Spirit yet, so he laid hands on them and they experienced his coming in power (Acts19:1-8). After this, for the next 2000 years, *every believer receives all* of the Holy Spirit and gifts there are for them at the time of conversion. A believer does not need to seek a "baptism of the Spirit and speak in tongues" to be a complete Christian (I Cor. 12:13), s/he needs only to cooperate with the Spirit to experience its fullness.

* We should take it as a warning that Simon believed and was baptized, but was not a *true* Christian. Peter perceived that he had never been converted. The same is true of many in our churches today. Paul issued a warning to the believers at Corinth: "Examine yourselves to see whether you are in the faith; test yourselves. Do you not realize that Christ Jesus is in you--unless, of course, you fail the test?" 2 Cor.13:5. Why did he say this? It was because they were *not acting like* what they claimed to be--new creations in Christ. We not only must examine ourselves, but we have a duty to question others who profess to be Christians but do not live like it.

26 MIRACLES DID HAPPEN

Read: Acts 9:32-43

In this passage it is obvious that Simon Peter has grown from an ordinary man into a spiritual giant.

After seeing what happened in Samaria, Peter decided to go out on mission to Lydda, a town on the Judean plain, to visit a group of believers. It was about twenty-nine miles northwest of Jerusalem. While there he healed a man named, Aeneas, who had been paralyzed for eight years. The effect was that many in the region turned to the Lord for salvation, which is the reason for the miracle.

A godly woman in Joppa died about this time. Joppa was a natural seaport on the Mediterranean coast, about 10 miles away. When believers there learned of Peter's presence in Lydda, they sent for him. Upon arrival he heard about the good works that Tabitha had done. Following the pattern of Jesus in raising Jairus' daughter (Mk.5:35-43) that he had witnessed, he sent everyone out of the room where the body was laid out, knelt down and prayed, and then said, "Tabitha, get up." He led her out of the room to her friends. And of course, the word of her resuscitation (she would die later) spread throughout the city and many came to believe in the Lord.

Application

* The believers at Joppa were *expecting* Peter to perform a miracle by raising Tabitha from the dead; that is why they sent for him. If God does not exist, miracles are impossible, but if He does, then He works through them to overcome the bias people have against believing in Him. The effect was that many believed in Christ, which is the purpose of miracles. Neither Jesus nor the apostles performed side show acts like those seen performed on television by Pentecostal

evangelists.

With the end of the Apostolic Age (100 AD), miracles like this *ceased*. They happen now only where people have never heard the Gospel in order to *attract* people to listen to the message of salvation.

Tabitha's resuscitation also pointed to the fact that all believers will be raised from the day when Christ returns in glory. All of the miracles that Jesus and the apostles did illustrate what it will be like when the Kingdom of God has come.

* The fact that the people in the church at Joppa showed Peter the good works that Tabitha had done indicates that she was *indispensible*. Some churches are dynamic because of *key* members. Someone said, "20% of members do 80% of the work in a church." As a pastor I have found that to be true. It doesn't take long for a pastor to learn whom he can depend on to get things done. Many of the members are just *spectators* and have no commitment to the future of the church. They attend worship with the same attitude as they do a sports event or outdoor concert (often wearing the same type clothing) or a show. They also attend in shifts: those in A show up every Sunday, those in B attend sporadically, and C group attends only special services. If the shifts are confused and all show up on the same Sunday then there is a crowd. In small congregations a core of five or six keep the church functioning. Tabitha must have been one of those persons.

* How was it that Phillip left Samaria for Gaza and Peter went to Lydda? An angel directed Phillip while Peter was *guided by circumstance*. Phillip witnessed to the Ethiopian eunuch, as Peter preached to Cornelius' family. The Lord knows which servant is best suited to do His work in different situations. Peter apparently was *free to go wherever he desired*. Can the Lord send an angel to direct us to a specific ministry? Yes. But it seems that He let me make my own decisions because

He has made me significant by giving me choices. How then is a believer to make everyday decisions if it is not by constantly second-guessing what the Lord's will might be? The biblical emphasis is on being a spiritually mature person and using the wisdom God has given in His word (e.g. Proverbs) to make everyday decisions. The Lord has told us to go, so if He does not prevent us from going where *we decide*, then we are operating in His sovereign will.

Any spiritually minded person can look back and discern how skills and experiences prepared him/her for the present place of service. I have often wondered why the Lord opened a door for me to minister in a certain church, but after being there several years or even after leaving, I can look back and see that my life and ministry met a need in that particular church.

* Later on, Peter believed the Lord gave him a ministry to the Jews and Paul was given a ministry to Gentiles (Acts 15:14 cf.Gal.2:8). This concept can prevent servants of God from being *jealous* or *envious* of one another's work.

27 A MOMENTOUS EVENT
Read: Acts 10:9-48

Caesarea was a Gentile city on the Mediterranean that served as a headquarters for the Roman government. Herod the Great spent twelve years and large amounts of money building a good harbor, an amphitheater and a pagan temple there. Cornelius was a

Roman centurion from Italy who had embraced the Jewish religion. (All the centurions mentioned in the NT are spoken well of.)

No doubt there were many centurions in Caesarea, but the Lord chose to send an angel to Cornelius because he was faithful to the revelation that he already had in Judaism. Peter was about 30 miles away at Joppa and was praying at noon, as was his Jewish custom. He was hungry and the Lord used it to give a vision of a sheet full of unclean animals coming down from heaven, commanding him to "kill and eat." Peter objected because the Levitical law forbade it. At the same time three messengers from Cornelius arrived and informed him that he was to travel with them to preach to Gentiles in Caesarea. A Jew was not even to enter the house of a Gentile. The favorite food of the Romans was pork, which caused great offense among the Jews. Peter is about to learn that the vision is not about eating unclean food; it is about all peoples now being offered salvation. The vision was repeated three times before he understood. Even then the Holy Spirit had to speak to him and tell him to go to the house of Cornelius.

Peter took six Jewish believers from the Joppa church along as witnesses (c.39 A.D.). When they arrived, they found Cornelius' house filled with his kinfolks and friends. Cornelius regarded Peter as a dignitary and bowed before him, to which Peter responded with telling him to stand up. (Why do people bow before the Pope and kiss his ring when not even Peter allowed such?) Cornelius related how an angel had instructed him to ask Peter to come and preach, which corroborated his vision.

The sermon was brief (vss.34-43) but contained the essence of the gospel. Suddenly, before he finished preaching, the Holy Spirit took over the service and the people began to speak in tongues, praising God (this is still the second phase of the gospel reaching Samaria). It was proof to Peter and his friends that God had accepted Gentiles on the same basis as he did the Jews at Pentecost, and the mixed-race Jews at Samaria. Then they immediately administered water baptism on these new believers.

Judaizers in the Jerusalem church heard what happened with the family and friends of Cornelius. Peter and the six men from the Joppa church went up to the church in Jerusalem to tell what the Lord had done in giving the Holy Spirit to the Gentiles. All those present agreed that this was a *new work* of the Lord that the church must accept (Acts 11:1-18).

Application

* This is one of the most *pivotal* events in Church history. The Jewish people knew they were special because they had a covenant relationship with God (Rom.9:4,5). As far as they were concerned there were only two groups of people, themselves and others. Everyone else was a Gentile and unacceptable to God (Eph.2:4,5). Peter held the typical Jewish view about Gentiles; this is why the Lord had to awaken him with a vision that Christianity was to include ethnic groups. Peter was prompted by the vision to exercise the "keys" to open the door of salvation to Gentiles. This *radically changed* the course of the Church because after this the gospel went to Gentiles as well as to Jews. The *theme* of the book of Acts, which covers the first forty years of Church history, is about why Christianity became a Gentile religion (Acts 28:28). If it had not broken out of the Jewish mold it would have been a sect of Judaism to this day. God clearly did a *new thing* by giving the Holy Spirit to Gentile believers and the church in Jerusalem knew it.

It is difficult for us to comprehend the attitude Jews had toward Gentiles, and vise versa. The Jewish people regarded the Gentiles as inferior and refused to mix with them. Gentiles despised the Jews because they thought they were arrogant and condescending toward them. Some of the historians of that time say that the Romans hated the Jews "because they hated all other people." It was amazing to the Jews that God would include such pagans in the New Covenant unless first making them follow the laws of the Old Covenant. Today, the Church is made up of people from all ethnic backgrounds because of this event.

* On this occasion the Holy Spirit spoke to Peter and gave him guidance. Was this a unique apostolic experience or the pattern every Christian should follow in order to know what to do?

* Peter has already expressed the *exclusivity* of belief in Jesus as necessary for salvation (4:12), so he is not contradicting it by saying that no matter what nation a person is from that, if s/ he fears God, they are acceptable to God (vss.34,35). Cornelius is an example of one who was obedient to the revelation he had, which prompted the Lord to provide a greater truth. General revelation includes God's work in the universe, nature, conscience, and providence. Special revelation includes: angels, theophanies (e.g. burning bush), prophets' writings, visions and dreams, miracles, tabernacle/Temple, and finally the Son of God (Heb.1:1-3). Cornelius was on the level of the writings of the Jewish prophets, but since God had sent his Son, he needed to hear and receive the *final* revelation in order to be saved (Acts 11:13,14).

The pagan has a *responsibility to seek* after the One True God and if he does, he will find Him. The problem is that people generally do not seek God because their sin nature blinds them (Ps.14:1-3). Unbelievers around the world who can learn the Gospel from radio, television, print, or at a local church who fail to do so are *fully responsible* for their own lost condition.

I'm convinced that any person living anywhere at any time, who is *faithful* to the revelation s/he has, that the Lord will provide the next level until he reaches the point of faith in Jesus Christ. Cornelius is an example of this truth. This would mean that before Jesus came the person's faith looked *forward* (e.g. Abraham was a Gentile pagan), but after Jesus came that faith looked *backward*, which would involve a missionary telling the story as Peter did with Cornelius. This principle has been verified many times in the history of Christian missions. (Read: ETERNITY IN THEIR HEARTS, by Don Richardson)

* Another statement in Peter's sermon needs explanation: After Jesus' resurrection ..."he was not seen by all the people, but by witnesses whom God had already chosen" vs.41. Why did Jesus not appear in his resurrection body to the Jewish and Roman leaders? He could have easily appeared at their residences and knocked on the door to announce that they had failed to be rid of him, but he did not do so. There are several possible answers. **First**, God gives only *sufficient* evidence for belief. He never overwhelms unbelievers because he respects their freedom. **Second**, Jesus had already given enough proof by his miracles and they had rejected them by claiming they were from the Devil (i.e. unpardonable sin). **Third**, if Jesus had shown himself to all the unbelievers in Jerusalem at one time they might have revolted against the Romans and tried to establish a political kingdom. John records that on one occasion the people tried to take Jesus and make Him king, but He slipped away (Jn.6:14,15). The kingdom Jesus wants to establish is spiritual, not physical. That can come about only by the present method of preaching the gospel and people accepting it one-by-one.

* Peter was wise to take along six men as witnesses. He must have anticipated that God was about to do something new among the Gentiles. The fact that he returned to Jerusalem to give a report indicates that he felt *accountable* to the Church (Acts 11:4). The critics of Peter (Judaizers) were not assured that what he did was right simply on the basis of his position of leadership in the Christian movement. Did they understand the radical nature of what had happened? Maybe so. They wanted to hear directly from Peter and make a decision themselves. It was only when he proved the immediate and manifest approval of God by Spirit baptism that they ceased their opposition, but only for a little while.

28 THE GREAT ESCAPE
Read: Acts 12:1-19

It is good when Roman history and Church history intersect. For example, the death of James the brother of John, and Herod Agrippa give us a time frame (41 to 44 A.D.) for events in the early church. During such instances, *faith* is connected with historical *facts*, making it more certain.

Because of Roman historians, we know much about the life of Herod Agrippa. He was the grandson of Herod the Great. He was born about 10 B.C. and was the son of Aristobulus and Bernice. He went to Rome after the death of his grandfather and remained there until around 30 A.D. He was a friend of Drusus, who was the son of Emperor Tiberius. He was banished from Rome and went to Palestine, taking an official post given him by his uncle Herod Antipas, which was about the time that Jesus was ministering in that region. Agrippa got into a conflict with his uncle and fled to Alexandria, where he borrowed money to go back to Rome to plead his case before the Senate. Emperor Caligula appointed him King of Trachonitis. Agrippa persuaded Caligula not to place a statue of himself in the Temple, which would have caused a revolt. In 41 A.D. when Claudius became Emperor, he was given rule over all the Jewish province.

Herod was proud of his Jewish heritage. In order

to gain popularity with the Jews in Jerusalem he decided to persecute the new sect (Christians) that was growing in popularity and irritating the Jews. He decided to use his political power to crush the Christians. (Politicians usually do anything to gain/stay in power.) Herod chose the most prominent and energetic champions of Christ to put to death, so James is beheaded.

This so pleased the Jewish authorities that Agrippa had Peter arrested and placed under Roman guards. (He had already escaped from Temple guards on previous arrests.) But an angel set Peter free and he went to the Upper Room (?) where the church had been in prayer for him. He told them to pass the word to James (the half-brother of Jesus), who was pastor of the Jerusalem church, that he was going into hiding until Herod dies (May, 44 A.D.). The next place we find Peter is in Antioch of Syria where Paul and Barnabas are ministering in a Gentile congregation (Gal.2:11-21).

Application

* The mother of James and John requested of Jesus that he let one sit on the right hand and the other on his left hand in glory (Mt.20:20-23). Jesus asked them, "Can you drink the cup I drink or be baptized with the baptism I am baptized with?" They answered, "We can." Then he told them that they would drink his cup and be baptized with his baptism. The request of this mother was fulfilled, in that, James was the first apostle to die a martyr's death and John was the last apostle to die a natural death.

* This is now the third imprisonment of Peter in Jerusalem. He will have one other in Rome. Suffering for the sake of Christ is the *normal* Christian life. All over the world Christians are being killed, especially in Muslim and Hindu countries. As Christians in America we have lived an *abnormal* Christian life because biblical principles have been so pervasive in our culture. We forget that many of our ancestors came to this

continent, not for riches, but for religious freedom. Because of Peter's own experiences he wrote about the suffering Christians should *expect* for doing what is right in a society where the majority is doing wrong (Read I Peter 4:12-19). Not only will Christians be persecuted by government policies and unbelievers, those who are faithful to the Scriptures will even suffer from others who profess to be Christians, and may even be scorned by their local church or their liberal denomination.

* The unbelief of the Christians that Peter had been delivered, in spite of their prayers, is humorous. The girl, Rhoda, was hysterical with joy and the group dismissed her claim that Peter is at the gate. The Lord set Peter free, not because of prayers of unbelief, but because it fit into God's eternal purpose, which cannot be thwarted by the acts of men or governments. We too are guilty of asking the Lord to work specifically in a case, and then when it happens we are surprised. It is sad that the 16 Roman soldiers, who must have had families, were possibly put to death because of Peter's deliverance, but it simply proves that the work of God is more important than the lives of any human being.

* It is a *mystery* as to why the Lord allowed James to be put to death, but he miraculously delivered Peter. James was part of the inner circle of Jesus' disciples, a key figure in the Jerusalem church. From the human perspective it makes no sense that the Lord would allow him to be executed. The only explanation is that he had *finished the work* the Lord had prepared for him (Eph.2:10). The church prayed, no doubt, as earnestly for James as it did for Peter, so it must have been the Lord's *sovereign will* for him to die this way.

29 PETER'S ENCOUNTERS WITH PAUL
Read: Galatians 1:18-2:14

Peter's *first encounter* with Paul was three years after the latter's conversion. Paul went immediately from Damascus into Arabia to rethink his theology; then he went to Jerusalem and spent fifteen days with Peter. The great apostle probably recounted the life of Christ for him so that Paul understood more completely the details of Jesus' ministry. The apostles then sent Paul to Tarsus, his hometown. This was in the year 33 A.D. (Gal. 2:1-10).

Fourteen years after his conversion, during Paul's ministry at the Antioch church, he and Barnabas took an offering (Acts 11:27-30) to the Jerusalem church (46 A.D.). They took Titus, a Gentile convert, to show how the gospel was being received among them. The Judaizers thought that Gentiles should be required to observe Jewish rituals, but Paul refuted this belief. Peter had his eyes opened to ministry among Gentiles in the Cornelius episode, so he could be receptive to Paul's work among them. At this *second encounter*, Peter, James and John approved of the work that Paul was doing among the Gentiles. Apparently, Peter had returned to Jerusalem after a brief ministry elsewhere, even though James, Jesus' half-brother was the leader of the church.

Peter went to Antioch (c. 47) to take part in the ministry to Gentiles (Gal.2:11-21). When he arrived, he participated in the social life of the Gentiles without hesitation. This was their *third* time together. Peter had no problem mixing with Gentile believers, until some of the Judaizers came from the Jerusalem church, then he pulled back. Paul confronted him before the whole church and charged him with being hypocritical, which he was. We are not told of Peter's reaction. He possibly went on mission to Upper Asia Minor and established churches (I Petr.1:1) while Paul and Barnabas were in Lower Asia Minor on their first mission. On his Second Missionary journey Paul was not allowed by the Spirit to preach in northern Asia Minor (Acts 16:6-8). Was this because Peter had already established a ministry there?

Paul and Barnabas returned to the church at Antioch after their first missionary journey and give a report of their success in establishing Gentile churches in southern Galatia (Acts 14:26-28). At the same time Judaizers were visiting these churches and teaching that a Gentile must first become a Jew and observe the Law before becoming a Christian. Paul wrote a harsh letter to the Galatian believers (from Corinth on his third journey) in which he pointed out that the Judaizers were preaching a *different* Gospel and not the one he preached to them (Gal.1:6-8; 4:8-11; 5:7-12; 6:12-16).

The issue of accepting Gentiles as full believers without becoming Jews had reached a crisis point. The only Apostolic Council ever called was a result of the incident with Peter at Antioch. The account is given in Acts 15:1-35. This took place in Jerusalem c.49 A.D. There is much debate as to whether the Council took place *before* or *after* Paul rebuked Peter because of his hypocrisy at Antioch. It must have been before the Council because I cannot accept that Peter would act contrary to the ruling at the Council.

With the apostles' present, Paul and Barnabas related how the Lord had worked through them to bring many Gentiles to salvation. After much heated discussion, Peter took a courageous stand. He declared that salvation is by grace alone apart from law keeping (vs.11). James then spoke up and reinforced Peter's statement by quoting an OT prophecy. This ended the discussion. The Council only advised in a letter to be read in Gentile churches to abstain from eating meat offered to idols, eating meat with blood in it, and maintaining sexual purity. This was the *fourth encounter* of Peter and Paul.

The *final meeting* of these two great apostles was in Rome c.64 A.D. (I Pet.5:13; Phil.4:22). Both were executed there within a few years.

Application

 * The biblical principle at work during these five encounters is: "As iron sharpens iron, so one man sharpens another" Prov.27:17. The interaction between them made them both better as apostles. They knocked the rough edges off one another as well as encouraged one another. They both grew in the Faith over the years. Second only to Jesus' conversation with the two disciples on the road to Emmaus, I would like to have listened in on the exchanges between Peter and Paul together. Peter probably related the historical events and teachings of Jesus, while Paul described his conversion and his struggle with Law and Grace. The questions and answers that flowed between them must have been rich with theological issues. They had to *reinterpret* all of their knowledge of the OT in light of Jesus being the Messiah.

 * These two giants of the Faith *complemented* one another's ministry when it would have been easy for them to be rivals for power. Peter ministered among the Jews and Paul among the Gentiles (Gal.2:8,9). If Peter had felt threatened by Paul's rise to fame, he could have destroyed his influence in the Christian movement and set it back for centuries. Instead, he helped Paul achieve great things for the Lord. Even though people in the church at Corinth compared the style of ministry these two apostles had and chose which one they preferred (I Cor.1:11,12), they never allowed it to divide them.

 * The Apostolic Council *defined the Gospel* once and for all time. If the Council had decided that Gentiles

must observe Jewish rituals to be Christians, the Gospel would have been distorted. Salvation would be by faith plus baptism, good works, church membership, etc. Even though it was settled that salvation is by grace through *faith alone* (Gal.2:14-16) there are denominations and churches that still teach other things must be *added* to faith. Many people live under these systems and cannot have assurance of salvation because they never know when they have done enough of this or that in order to be acceptable to God.

In churches and denominations today politics play a major role among pastors. When they come together for a meeting they are always looking over the shoulders of the person they are talking to in order to see someone that can help them climb to the top. These are unwritten signals and codes, but most pastors know how to play the game. Those who are successful are often the ones that get the larger church or a better position in the denominational organization. Seldom is there any openness between pastors for fear of being stabbed in the back. I was ready to do the politicking when I graduated from seminary, but I was spared by a *series of fortunate circumstances*. I was in a situation where I was wounded deeply and surrounding pastors turned theirs backs. Only 2 or 3 in the area came to my side to encourage me. After that experience I did not rely on the good-old-boy system to secure a pastorate. If the Lord did not open a door to a church, I was willing to do something else, and I did. I have never been out of a pastorate for more than a few months over fifty years of ministry.

30 PETER'S LEGACY
Read: Jn.21:18-23

In a post-resurrection appearance, Jesus told Peter that he would be arrested and put to death against his will when he was an old man. Peter was naturally curious about how John's life would end because they had bonded together during Jesus' three years of ministry. Jesus in essence said, "That is not for you to know." Peter had not lost his tendency to be inquisitive. Jesus then was very direct about Peter's mission: "You must follow me."

During Nero's persecution Peter was crucified along with his wife (c.66 A.D.). This is not recorded in the NT, but there are numerous references in the Church Fathers. Lactantius wrote in 320 A.D. "While Nero reigned, the apostle Peter came to Rome. Through the power of God committed to him, he worked certain miracles. And by turning many to the truth, he built up a faithful and steadfast church to the Lord...It was Nero who had Peter crucified..." What of Peter's wife? We do not even know her name or anything about her. Yet, Clement of Alexandria (195 A.D.) wrote: "Peter, on seeing his wife led to death, rejoiced on account of her call to go home, shouting to her very encouragingly and comfortingly by name and saying, 'Remember the Lord!' Such was the marriage of the blessed apostle." It must have been like the marriage he described of a godly wife and husband (I Pet.3:1-7). Nothing is known of where she is buried.

What were the circumstances that led to the death of Peter and his wife in Rome? Peter had been arrested twice and had to defend himself before the Sanhedrin. In addition he was arrested and placed in Antonia Tower prison by Herod Agrippa and threatened with death, but an angel delivered him. The church itself was experiencing persecution from the Jews in

Jerusalem, so Peter and his wife probably left after the Apostolic Council in 49 A.D. We know that they traveled to Corinth on mission before Paul wrote to them in 55 A.D. because he alludes to it (I Cor.1:12; 9:5). By the time of his death Peter had been preaching sedition against Rome by declaring that Christians are "a holy nation, a people belonging to God...as alien and strangers in the world...live such good lives among the pagans" I Pet. 2:9b,11a,12a. What would this kind of language sound like to Roman officials? Rebellion.

Peter wrote two, and possibly three letters while he was in Rome, to the churches he had established in Upper Asia Minor. The themes of these letters are encouragement of believers to face persecution, a warning about false teachers (2 Pet.2) and the second coming of Christ (2 Pet.3:1-13). Some find a third letter attached to his first letter (chapter 4:12-5:14). It was probably placed at the end by a copyist because it connects with the statements about suffering. There is no indication that Peter and his wife ever returned to Jerusalem.

By the early 60s A.D. they were in Rome (I Pet.5:12,13). Peter identified himself as an elder, not as the bishop of Rome (1 Pet.5:1,2). The Roman Church claims that it has Peter's wooden bishop's chair in the Basilica of the Vatican, however, he did not elevate himself above Paul, for he was familiar with his writings, which he equated with the OT Scriptures (2 Pet. 3:15,16). This statement shows that he held Paul in high esteem.

Application

    * Peter and his wife were *faithful* servants of the Lord. We don't know whether she traveled with him on every mission or if she stayed in Galilee. They probably did not have any children because he does not allude to them in his letters. Either way, his wife made great sacrifices so that he could be an effective servant of the

Lord. Throughout church history there have been many wives of pastors, evangelists, and missionaries who have served behind the scenes to make their husband's ministry successful.

My wife and I met and married our last year in college. She then taught school to put me through seminary, and continued teaching for 45 more years to supplement my income from small churches. She sang in the choir, played the piano, taught youth classes, and visited the sick to take food. This was her role in ministry. On the personal level, she fulfilled the duties of a wife and mother without complaint. Behind the scenes she was an encourager when I was discouraged. A few years ago, I asked her if she was able to separate the man in the pulpit from the man she lived with everyday; she said, "Yes." (Imagine listening to the same preacher for 50 years and knowing all of his weaknesses.) She also suffered when church members were hurtful in their comments and actions. Her rewards in Heaven will be great.

* Peter probably reflected in these later years on the *providence of God* in his life. The Lord had told him that when he was an old man he would be put to death, but the Lord did not tell him when and where. It is common in the midst of life to wonder what the Lord is doing in and through us, but it is only near the end that we can look back and see the hand of God in what has happened. There is a sense of peace that comes in the later years when one has been faithful through all the ups and downs of ministry. I have reached that place, and it is glorious.

* Ironically, Peter (and his wife?) were put to death by the very government that he had instructed Christians to submit to (I Pet.2:13,14). Nero was one of the most wicked Caesars of all. He probably set fire to the city of Rome. Christians were his scapegoat. Thousands were rounded up and put to death, including

Peter and Paul. There was no deliverance this time, as had happened on previous occasions, because their work was finished, and they knew it (2 Tim. 4:6-8).

As Peter aged he probably realized that the Roman government would persecute Christians. He believed that Rome had lost its divine mandate to govern for good. It was corrupt to the core and must be resisted. He did not, however, counsel that Christians should take up arms. This was wise because the Roman army was so powerful that they would have been destroyed. Neither did he advise *anarchy*. This happens when each person does whatever he chooses. If man were basically good, this would work. But because humanity is fallen; men will not do what is best for themselves and their neighbors if there is no government to enforce just laws (I Tim.1:8-11). Evidence of this is seen in places where governments have failed: chaos, riots, murder, looting, and destruction happens. Peter must have used evasive tactics to avoid confrontation with Roman authorities for the last 20 years of his life; this was wise. At the time of their death, both Peter and Paul were in their late 60s.

Our Founding Fathers recognized the *sinful nature of humanity* and established a government with checks and balances. Even at that, corruption and partisanship have crept in so that our government is promoting injustice and sinfulness. The first Amendment is supposed to guarantee the "free exercise of religion" but this is being interpreted by the government to mean only inside the four walls of the church.

Christians especially no longer have the favor of government because we oppose its policies (approval of gambling, abortion, homosexuality, redistribution of goods through unjust taxes, spying on political conservatives, forcing businesses to serve homosexuals, etc.). This present government has targeted Christian churches, organizations and institutions for harassment. Is taxation of church property next? Will preaching against sin be labeled as "hate speech" as it is now in England and Canada? We must oppose an oppressive government and take the consequences. It has reached the point that we should begin saluting the Christian flag rather than the national flag.

CONCLUSION

In 846 a Muslim force of 73 ships, with 11,000 soldiers and 500 horses attacked Rome. The tombs of Peter and Paul were desecrated and their respective Basilicas sacked. The altar covering the body of Peter was smashed. The invasions of Spain, Italy, and France at this time led to the Europeans *responding* with the Crusades 200 years later.

During WW2 the Roman Church excavated under the Vatican and found a box that contained the bones of a large man, about 70 years of age, wrapped in a purple robe with gold thread. They conjecture that it is the remains of the apostle Peter, so that allegedly the Vatican is built on the Rock. Today, visitors can go down into a crypt and see the box behind glass. Above it inscribed in Greek is: "Peter is buried here." It is more likely the bones of one of the later Popes.

There is little doubt that Peter led the church at Rome until his death in 66 A.D. He was the *most influential* of the Twelve Disciples. Even with all of his failings he became a great servant of our Lord Christ. He is truly an example of the folk saying that "God can hit a straight lick with a crooked stick." He was worthy of being designated "The Rock" because he certainly stood firm to the end. We can honor him without exalting him as done by the Roman Catholic or the Easter Orthodox churches.

118

Appendix—

Analysis of the First Letter

1:1,2 Salutation.
  3-12, Future glory makes present suffering light.
  13-25, Therefore, they should live holy lives.
2:1-10, They should realize the high calling they received.
  11-12, Their lives should expose Gentile lies.
  13-17, They should be loyal citizens.
  18-25, Be good and patient servants, as Christ was.
3:1-6, Wives are to be chaste and modest.
  7, Men are to be considerate husbands.
  8-19, Clear in conscience; suffer for doing right.
  20-22. Rescued by baptism, like Noah in flood.
4:1-6, No longer libertines like Gentiles.
  7-11a, Exercise of Spiritual Gifts
  11b, Doxology

Analysis of the Second Letter

1:1,2, Salutation.
  3,4, Exhortation to grow in Christian graces
  5-11, Progress in Christian growth.
  12-18, Eye witness to Transfiguration.
  19-21, Confirmed by prophecy.
2:1-9, Beware of false teachers whose end will be like the rebellious angels.
  10-21, Corrupters and corrupt; like Balaam, insolent, and licentious.
3:1-4, Further warning against those who doubt the Second Coming.
  5-10, Which nevertheless is certain.
  11-14, And serves as a strong motive for holy living.
  15,16, As Paul teaches in all his letters.
  17,18, Final warning to guard against false teachers.

Analysis of Possible Third Letter

(Written while awaiting crucifixion c.66 A.D.)
I Peter 4:12, Salutation.
   4:13-19, Suffering is to be expected and endured.
5:1-6, Elders must be faithful shepherds to their flock.
   7-9, Satan is a deadly enemy to be resisted.
   10,11, Christ will strengthen them to endure
      suffering.
   12, Silvanus is secretary of this short, encouraging
      letter.
   13, Church in Rome is sister to churches in
      Asian provinces (I Pet. 1:1)
   14, Final farewell.

Made in the USA
Coppell, TX
27 May 2024

32842045R00073